THE PARSON PREACHING

The Parson Preaching

By the Reverend
CLEMENT F. ROGERS, M.A.

Professor Emeritus of Pastoral Theology
King's College, University of London

LONDON

S·P·C·K

1947

"On publie pour les amis inconnus."
Flaubert, *Correspondence*, Vol. II
(Paris, Charpentier, 1894), p. 82.

MADE IN GREAT BRITAIN

" The Countrey Parson preacheth constantly. The pulpit is his joy and his throne: if he at any time intermit, it is either for want of health, or against some, Festival that he may the better celebrate it, or for the variety of the hearers, that he may be heard at his returne more attentively.—When he preacheth, he procures attention by all possible art."—George Herbert, *A Priest to the Temple or the Countrey Parson.* Chapter VII, " The Parson Preaching."

CONTENTS

PAGE

PREFACE xi

INTRODUCTION xiii

Changed condition of Preaching to-day—Books on Homiletics
by great preachers—the needs of the ordinary man and of the
student—teaching in a Theological College.

CHAP.

I. THE COLLECTION OF MATERIAL 1

(i) More than a week necessary for preparation—" preaching
on the Gospel for the day "—danger of a desultory habit of
mind—ideas coming at odd moments—to be written down at
once—carry about a note-book—each entry to be on a separate
sheet—loose-leaf note-books—enter full references—abbreviations and symbols—each entry under a heading.

(ii) Material—these the ideas that are your own—new ideas—
quotations—illustrations—stories—need of collecting material
beforehand.

(iii) Sorting and filing—go through entries at leisure—some
entered or torn up at once—others filed—analyses of books—
separate the material for preaching—sermons gradually forming
themselves—the basis of regular study and note-taking.

II. THE COMPOSITION OF THE SERMON . . . 18

The Psychology of Thought—three elements, sight, sound and
words—the physical basis in brain-centres—first see your
sermon.
(i) The shape of the composition—what makes a pattern—
sight and lucidity—balance and proportion—make an outline—
terseness of expression—the paragraph.

(ii) What is the pattern to be ?—The " Rule of Three "—in
objects of sight—in pictures—in music—in verse—in Grammar
and Logic—in Drama—in practical life—variety in power of
visualising—the Herbartian Method in Education—see your
sermon in an outline of three parts—the Introduction and
Presentation of the Subject—The Middle, the appeal to the
intellect—the End, the lesson to be learned—get unity by a
Title—Point by a definite aim.

(iii) The element of Sound—keeping to the outline—imagine an audience as present—things heard and things read—variety of tone—re-enacting in the pulpit what was written at the desk—" Style is the Man himself."

III. THE STORAGE OF MATERIAL . . . 40

Material growing continually—planning ahead.
(i) The need for the preacher—little can be got into one sermon—casual labour and high-class work—the single sermon —ideas recurring from reading—sermons in groups of three or four—concentration on essentials—supplementing by school work —by parish work—by literature.

(ii) Value to the preacher himself—continuity and coherence —stimulus to study—note taking in reading—an education in proportion and breadth—dealing with subjects thoroughly— preventing omissions—a plan for three months ahead—a plan if single-handed—various types of sermons—his theological out-look organised—learning by teaching.

(iii) Value for the congregation—the regular and the occasional churchgoers—the preacher putting himself in their place—what they should have heard in a year—subjects they never hear treated—indirectly reaching people who never come to church.

(iv) The opportunities of the pulpit—effectiveness hindered by little things.

IV. THE DELIVERY OF SERMONS . . . 64

The place of Sound in Thought—reading by the eye insufficient— the genius of the English Language—complaints of inaudibility —the Science of Phonetics—the need of self-teaching.

(i) Differences in expression altering meaning—examples from the Book of Common Prayer—need of control of accent—of tone of the voice—interest in the subject the first need—a course at a Theological College—practice on secular poetry—choice of pieces—the first aim, to get mouth-consciousness—listening to and thinking about elocution.

(ii) Speech as an Art—effect of continuous sub-conscious criticism—in conversation—in common worship—of practice in singing—result seen later—practice in a large hall—over passages from Shakespere—correcting by Phonetics.

(iii) Practice in a Church—learning to increase voice—vigour by restraint—in the pulpit—at the lectern—in the choir-stall—the said service—the sung service—at the altar—different ways of saying the same words.

(iv) Books on preaching—chief value when actually at work— the Future of English—the part played by the Pulpit.

APPENDICIES

		PAGE
I.	HYMN SINGING	86
II.	BUFFON ON STYLE	89
III.	SUBJECTS FOR SERMONS FOR THREE MONTHS AHEAD	94
IV.	A THREE MONTHS' PLAN FOR SERMONS THREE TIMES A WEEK	97
V.	SUBJECTS ASKED FOR BY SOLDIERS AT A " PADRE'S HOUR "	99
VI.	THE LEGITIMATE USE OF THE SERMONS OF OTHERS	102
VII.	ABSTRACT AND CONCRETE OR GENERALS AND PARTICULARS	106
VIII.	SUBJECTS OF SUNDAY AFTERNOON LECTURES IN HYDE PARK	115
IX.	THE LITERATURE OF PREACHING	117
	INDEX	126

PREFACE

SIR THOMAS BROWNE, so we are told, lamented the loss of his library. There were no " good bookes," that is to say, no books which enshrined the heavy learning of Europe, on his shelves at Shipton Hall. So, too, Jeremy Taylor, a year or two later, bemoaned his misfortune at having to write his *Liberty of Prophesying* away from his library. " Neither of these great authors," says Mr. Edmund Gosse, " appreciated the immense advantage they gained from being torn from their traditional support and being made to depend on their imagination and memory."

I do not claim to be a great author, but I sympathise with their complaints and ask for the forbearance of my readers. Under the circumstances produced by the War I would fain believe that my imagination has been stimulated and my memory strengthened. But I fear it is not so. I must, therefore, ask those who read what I have written to be kind in their judgement if, like Jeremy Taylor, I have tried to divert my thoughts " from the perpetual meditation of my private troubles and the public duscrasy." People have been more than kind in giving me shelter, but I have not found that it has made it easier to write if you are away from your books, or that it stimulates your imagination to prove, with Dante, how salt is " the savour of another's bread " nor,

> " How hard the passage to descend and climb
>   By others' stairs,"

to say nothing of the difficulties of paper- and labour-shortage and the reluctance of publishers to undertake new ventures in print. But at least I have been supported by Memory and what I have written has been based upon what we built up at King's College in London after the war of 1914–18. Circumstances are much the same now as they were then, when a former generation faced so wonderfully a state of things so similar. The Pulpit still has wonderful opportunities which I should wish to help the newly ordained, as well as veterans in the service of the Church, to make the most of to-day.

For it is my firm conviction that the ultimate solution of all our problems lies in the Christian Faith. Our troubles in Europe are, in the last resort, due to our failure to build up our civilisation on Christian ideas. Our difficulties in India are due to fundamental contrast of Pantheistic Hinduism and its practical Polytheism and Unitarian Islam and its Fatalism. Our hopes in Africa in the future depend on whether Paganism or Christianity is to prevail; in the whole world of men in their learning " How beautiful a thing it is, Brethren, to dwell together in unity."

And the Pulpit is an important factor in the contest. It appeals to the ordinary man on whom so much depends. It would be a pity if its opportunities were thwarted by trivial mistakes in the composition and delivery of Sermons, by wrong methods of composition and delivery.

CLEMENT F. ROGERS.

89 *Woodstock Road,*
   Oxford.
      March 11, 1947.

INTRODUCTION

No apology is needed for another book on sermon-writing, nor need we waste time in stressing the difficulties of preaching. Many books have been written on the subject, but few of them are of much use to the beginner. They have mostly been written by famous preachers who have been asked to give a course of lectures to students and have afterwards published what they wrote to deliver; but in most cases they were delivered in an age when preaching took a different place in public life. Sermons were then longer and formed the chief feature of public worship. They were really more in the nature of lectures, and generally lasted the best part of an hour. Nowadays the ordinary sermon is a single item in the whole complex of a liturgy, though perhaps not less important on that account.

Moreover, the task of famous preachers is different from that which lies before the student in the theological college or the priest of the ordinary parish, and it is doubtful whether the great man's special qualifications really help him to be of much use to the less gifted. Besides, he is so used to preaching in the pulpit that he continues to preach from the lecture-desk, and in a book writes " oratoriously ".[1] It is really of no use to say that " men should write their own sermons "; that they should be " in the genuine language of the preacher's heart "; that he should " acquire a natural manner ", that " the sermon should explain a text ", and "should give its sense"; that the preacher "should be nice, sober, and chaste "; that his preaching should not be " overcharged with diction " (nothing should be *over*charged with anything). Nor is it useful to say that " prayer is the foundation of preaching "; that " the text should be thoughtfully chosen"; that the preacher " should make his meaning clear "; or that " he must know when to stop ". It is all perfectly true, and we all know it is true, and we could all say it to ourselves, without a famous preacher coming to say it to us. But it doesn't help us in the least to write or to preach a sermon.

[1] John Selden (1584–1654), *Table Talk*, Sec. 81: " The Fathers at times speak oratoriously."

The great preacher finds that preaching comes naturally to him, and seldom needs to examine closely how it should be done. He repeats the experience of others, and by the practice of rhetoric has often good things to say about the science that has been built up in the schools. But this has all been better done by the master mind of Aristotle analysing the practice of the Athenian law courts, by Cicero explaining his practical methods as summed up in the commonplaces of the rhetoricians of his day; by Quintilian as an element in education; by Augustine using his experience in teaching students at Rome and Milan and in his application of it to the clergy of Africa to guide them *de Doctrina Christiana* in Christian teaching; or by men, like Whately, who approach homiletics as a special branch of the larger general study of rhetoric and elocution, though writing " principally for the instruction of *unpractised* writers." [1] But all these, while perhaps useful to the man already engaged in preaching, if only to make him reflect on what he is doing and to keep up his interest in doing it well, are of little help to the ordinary student, who needs training in first principles and guidance in practice. Science always comes after experience. What the beginner needs is help to start on right lines and to be kept from wrong ways from the first.

It has been my good fortune to have had to face this problem in one of England's best schools for training for the Ministry. At King's College we had a three years' course in theology, taken after a preliminary year for those for whom it was needed. Besides their study of theology, the minds of students were directed to its practical application in life, and Pastoral Theology included the study of how to apply it in preaching and in the delivery of sermons. What follows is based on my experience there with first- and third-year men. The readers I have in mind are the men in our Theological Colleges, though I hope I may find others among the ordained clergy and among lay-readers. I believe, too, that the principles I have stressed and the methods I have advised may be useful also to school-teachers and writers of the popular theology which is so much needed to-day by the ordinary man.

---

[1] *Elements of Rhetoric*, Preface.

I

COLLECTION OF MATERIAL

" In making a speech one must study three points. First, the means of producing persuasion ; second, the style, or language to be used ; and, thirdly, the proper arrangement of the various parts of the speech."—
Aristotle, *Rhetoric*, Bk III, 1, tr. W. Rhys Roberts (Oxford, 1924).

" My tables—meet it is I set it down."
—Shakespeare, *Hamlet*, Act. I, Sc. 5.

" When found, make a note of."—Captain Cuttle, *Dombey and Son*, Ch. XV.

" Ere the passing hour go by
Quick, thy tablets, Memory."
—Matthew Arnold, " A Memory Picture ", *Poetical Works* (Macmillan, 1890), p. 23.

THE first thing to realise in the making of sermons is that it takes more time than we think. Not necessarily more work. Indeed, if we spread our work over a longer span, the labour of composition will be much less. If we give them time to incubate, our thoughts will come of themselves and will shape themselves without trouble. The greater part of the process will be unconscious and automatic. *It is impossible to make up a good sermon in a week.*

It is important for the student to realise this while still at College, for on getting to his parish he will find little to encourage him to work intelligently and according to the laws of thought. He will almost certainly find it assumed that in a " well-organised parish " it is the custom to " meet on Monday to arrange the work for the week ". It is assumed that nothing is arranged more than seven days ahead, in spite of the fact that the arrangements for the coming week have already been announced in church the day before and can be altered only at great inconvenience. The consequence is that there is no continuity or plan in the work, except that which the individual makes for himself in spite of the system. The whole pressure of custom intensifies the natural propensity of most men to live from hand to mouth—a bad habit which characterises the lowest and most unintelligent kinds of casual labour. Fancy what would happen if a school or college were run on such a principle ! There could be no syllabus of work. The masters could teach nothing continuous, and would become exhausted by the daily labour of preparing lessons overnight. The boys or students would learn nothing, but would be confused and trained to think with a desultory habit of mind. Yet such is the weight of a foolish tradition that an acute and clear thinker like Mr. Graham Wallas, in explaining the necessity of taking a longer time over things and examining their psychological foundations, can quote as an example that of " a well-known academic psychologist who was also a preacher ", who told him :—

> " That he found by experience that his Sunday sermon was much better if he posed the problem on Monday than if he did so later in the week, although he might give the same number of hours of conscious work to it in each case." [1]

But how much better still it would have been, with even less conscious work, in a month!

The result is that a large number of our preachers get into the habit of " preaching on the Gospel for the day ". This in itself is not a mistake, for the Epistles and Gospels, with the round of Fasts and Feasts in the Calendar, form quite a good syllabus of preaching for a year. Editions of the *Catechism of the Council of Trent* are issued by the authorities of the Roman Church with outlines for sermons, with back-references to the Catechism, for each Sunday of the year. But the ordinary man does not look so far ahead, and probably

[1] *The Art of Thought* (Cape, 1927), p. 86. He continues : " It seems to be a tradition among practising barristers to put off any consideration of each brief to the latest possible moment before they have to deal with it. This fact may help to explain a certain want of depth which has often been noticed in the typical lawyer-statesman, and which may be due to his conscious thought not being sufficiently extended and enriched by subconscious thought."

Cp. p. 147. " Weekly journalism, where a man has two or three, or even four or five days between the choice of his subject and the completion of his article, is far less dangerous to thought than daily journalism, and monthly and quarterly journalism has often been one of the ways in which the most patient thinkers have discovered and published their results."

(And, we may add, some of your best " original " ideas you often find there already in reading sermons you wrote thirty or forty years ago.)

Cp. my *Pastoral Theology and the Modern World* (Oxford, 1920), Ch. I, " The Span of Work ", pp. 1–3.

Progress in civilisation has been largely due to increase in man's power to look ahead. . . .

Class differences, with their contrasts in personal dignity of life, are directly dependent on the length of the span of work done by men. . . .

The type of man, and the value of what he does, is bound up with the length of his unit of work. How is it with the clergy and what they do?

I have there dealt with the question at greater length and in relation to the whole of his work, and not merely to that of preaching.

takes his " day off " on Tuesday after the meeting on Monday, and only begins to get down to his sermon on Wednesday.

So he also begins to worry and ask himself what there is in the Gospel for the next Sunday that he can talk about. In the old days of horse-trams it was said that it was the starting of the trams that wore out the horses; when once they were got going it was easy enough work for them. But the preacher has the continuous weekly strain to meet, so that " The Parson's Perplexity—What Shall I Preach About? " has become an advertisement headline. The line of least resistance is that of talking ready-made platitudes—a course fatally tempting to follow. It is not so difficult to string together sentences full of abstract words ending in " -ion "—words which perhaps mean something to the preacher, but nothing to the congregation till they have in their minds the concrete instances from which they are abstracted.[1] There are men and women, it has been said with truth, who have listened to hundreds of sermons, but who if stopped at the church door and asked one by one why they believed in God, would in nine cases out of ten be unable to give an answer.

No! Knowledge takes longer to mature. A recent writer in the *Spectator*[2] told of the delight of a young man in the Army who, when he heard a sermon on " How the Gospels were Written ", declared that it was the first time he had heard " anyone advance a reason to believe the Bible might be true ". No doubt the majority of our preachers have " got up the Synoptic Problem " for their ordination examination, but they could not in a week select the chief points, decide what they must leave out, arrange their matter

---

[1] Cp. Jeremy Taylor, *Works* (London, 1854), Vol. I, p. 107. " Rules and Advice to the Clergy of the Diocese of Down and Connor for their deportment in their personal and public Capacities. IV. Rules and Advice concerning preaching," xlii : " Do not spend your sermons in general and indefinite things, as in exhortations to people to get Christ, to be united to Christ, and things of like unlimited signification, but tell them in every duty which are the measures, what circumstances, what instruments, and what is the particular minute meaning of every general advice. For generals not explicated do but fill people's heads with empty notions, and their mouths with perpetual unintelligible talk, and themselves are not edified."

Cp. GeorgeHerbert, *A Priest to the Temple or the Countrey Parson*. Ch. XXVI, " The Parson's Eye ". " Country people are . . . cunning to make use of another and spare themselves. And Scholars ought to be diligent in the observance of these, and driving of their general Schoole rules ever to the smallest actions of life; which while they dwell in their bookes, they will never find; but being seated in the Countrey, and doing their duty faithfully, they will soon discover: especially if they carry their eyes open, and fix them on their charge and not on their preferments."

[2] December 11th, 1942.

B

to make it clear and interesting, and write it out in the speech of everyday life. So people never hear why we believe the Gospels to contain genuine history, and have nothing to say when they hear it asserted that they were written halfway through the second century. This living from hand to mouth extends to all kinds of parish work.

But the young curate will not be able to alter it, and any suggestion will be regarded, and resented, as criticism. Unless he takes care, he will come to acquiesce in this desultory habit of mind. So let him store up in his memory what he finds, and organise ahead for himself. He will know roughly how often he will have to preach in the next month—in the next three months—and can form a general idea for the next six months or for the year. Let him study the laws of thought and realise how he can get something to say. *Let him set up for himself the mechanism for reasoning and for securing the ideas that come to him.*

I

They come as the result of steady work. How to read he should have learned at College. He should have been made familiar with the outlines of theology, so that it has become systematised for him. He cannot there read everything even in outline, but he should come away knowing what gaps he has still to fill in, what parts he has so far merely got from lectures and still needs to make his own by reference to good or, where possible, to first-hand authorities. He should have learned to verify his references.[1] He should be familiar with the titles of the best books and be able to judge of the authority of authors. He has plenty of time for reading before him if he looks ahead, even if he has not much time each day. He should have formed habits of reading, and should at once set about forming such new habits as are possible in his circumstances. " It only needs ", said Joubert, " a moment for sagacity to get a picture of the whole ; it needs years of exactness to work it all out." [2]

It is in such hours of serious study that new ideas are acquired, but they have to be " marked, learned, and inwardly digested ". This is, for the most part, an unconscious process. We learn, as has been pointed out, to swim in winter and to skate in summer.

[1] For Dr. Routh's advice to Dean Burgon see the preface to my *Verify Your References* (S.P.C.K., 1938), p. v.

[2] *Pensées*, Titre XXIII, 50: " Il ne faut qu'un moment à la sagacité pour tout apercevoir ; il faut des années à l'exactitude pour tout exprimer."

Cp. No. 52: " Le génie commence les beaux ouvrages, mais le travail seul les achève " (Genius begins beautiful works, but only labour completes them).

There is need of incubation. When we relax our efforts the brain takes up the work, and without fatigue carries on the task automatically. Taking exercise, not too violent or fatiguing, is not a waste of time; it is part of the process of learning.

For ideas come to us at odd moments, of themselves, without effort on our part, as the result of effort in the past. Their coming depends on our mood, on accidents of circumstances, on chance reading or conversation, on our state of health at different times of the day. They suddenly emerge from our subconsciousness, and may not come again. Such are the ideas that interest us, that we have made our own, and therefore it is likely that they will interest others when we tell them. Much of what I am writing now has become my own as the result, I see now, of reading Mr. Graham Wallas' book *The Art of Thought* and other books a good many years ago. He points out how what he calls " fringe thoughts " come into our minds suddenly when we are engaged in our ordinary work. " In modern life ", he writes :—.

> " the range of observation and memory which may start a new thought-train is so vast that it is almost incredibly easy to forget some thought and never pick up the trail which led to it. The story may be true which tells of a man who had so brilliant an idea that he went into the garden to thank God for it and found on rising from his knees that he had forgotten it and never recalled it. And if a thinker is fortunate enough to be visited by some large conception—a constructive theory, or a story or poem—which carries with it from the first an intimation of its complete form, he must break through all his habits and duties till the impulse to develop and record it is exhausted." [1]

Put down these thoughts at once. They may not come again, at any rate without your racking your brain to remember what they were. They may easily be lost.

John Aubrey in his " Brief Life " of Hobbes, that master of clear and original, if often mistaken, thought, tells us that he

> " walked much and contemplated and he had in the head of his staffe a pen and inke-horn, carried alwayes a note book in his pocket, and as soon as a thought darted, he presently entered it into his booke, or otherwise he might perhaps have lost it." [2]

[1] *Op. cit.*, Ch. VI, " Thought and Habit ". The whole book, to which I am deeply indebted for all this section, should be read.

[2] *Brief Lives, chiefly of Contemporaries, set down by John Aubrey between the years 1669–1696.* Edited from the Author's MSS. by Andrew Clark (Oxford, 1898), Vol. I, p. 334.

" Presently " means, of course, " immediately ", and not after a little time, as our habits of procrastination have led us to use the word.

St. Anselm, so his biographer Eadmer tells us, set himself to frame one single and short answer to prove the belief and preaching of the Church about God—that He is eternal, unchangeable, almighty, incomprehensible, just, holy, merciful, true; and the Truth, Goodness, and Justice, and more, how these were all one in Him. The problem worried him at meals and in his sleep; it distracted him at Matins and at Mass, till he began to wonder whether it were not a temptation from the Devil. Then one night between the vigils the grace of God shone in his heart and the matter became clear to his intellect, and a great joy and rejoicing filled his heart. So he wrote it down at once on his wax tablets and gave them to one of the brothers to keep carefully. On asking for them a few days later they were not to be found. He re-wrote something of his former notes and again gave them to the monk with special caution to take care of them. He hid them in his bed, but the next day the wax was found to be broken. St. Anselm pieced them together carefully, and though he recovered practically all that he had written, he would not run the risk of losing it again, and ordered it to be written down on parchment. Had it been lost he might never have written his *Proslogion !* [1]   And the moral of that is, as the Duchess would have told Alice, that *it will not do to make notes on backs of envelopes or on stray pieces of paper that you may happen to have in your pocket.* Except, of course, in cases of absolute necessity. There is a story told by the Chevalier de Méré which almost certainly refers to his first meeting with Pascal. The Chevalier was from the first struck with the few sayings the perhaps rather silent and, as he thought, awkward young man uttered from time to time, but was apparently still more impressed by the fact that he was not merely a good listener. That always impresses talkers, and the young Pascal did not merely listen. Like Hamlet, " il avait des tablettes ", and when the great man said something specially striking he pulled them out and made a note of it.[2] In later years he developed this practice, and his

[1] *Vita Sancti Ambrosii,* Cap. II, 26; M.P.L. 138, col. 63.

[2] Pascal, *Pensées,* ed. Brunschvicg (Paris, Hachette, 1922), p. 115, "Deux ou trois jours s'étant écoulés de la sorte, il eut quelque défiance de ses sentiments, et ne faisant plus qu'écouter ou qu'interroger, pour s'éclaircir sur les sujets qui se présentaient, il avait des tablettes qu'il tirait de temps en temps, où il mettait quelque observation." (After two or three days had passed in this way he got a certain mistrust of his own ideas and only listened or asked questions and to clear his mind on the subject, he had a note-book which he drew out from time to time in which he put down some remark.)

note-books were the basis of his *Provincial Letters* and of his never-written *Apology*. The notes for the latter were published later as his *Thoughts* or *Pensées*, perhaps the greatest work in all French literature, but many of his thoughts, like those of Hobbes, " darted " at inconvenient times, and he had to write them down on such scraps of paper as he happened to have on him, sometimes even, as Nicole tells us,

" he came back from his walk with his nails covered with signs (*charactères*) which he had scratched on them with a pin, signs which recalled to his mind thoughts which might have been otherwise lost to him so that this great man came home like a bee laden with honey." [1]

So, too, when Henri Poincaré was working at a difficult problem about Fuchsian functions he found that his investigations were leading to nothing, so he went off for a few days to the seaside and banished mathematics, as he supposed, from his thoughts. But suddenly he was stung by the splendour of a sudden thought that " the arithmetical transformations of indefinite ternary quadratic forms are identical with those of non-Euclidean Geometry " ! [2]

We cannot all expect such inspirations of Truth, but A. E. Housman has told us how he wrote *A Shropshire Lad*. As he took his

[1] Cp. Sainte Beuve, *Port Royal* (7th Ed., Paris, 1922), Vol. IV, p. 599, quoting from a manuscript of uncertain authorship belonging to some Dutch friends of his : " A l'occasion de M. Pascal, je (me) rapelle que M. Nicole m'a dit que quelquefois il revenoit de la promenade avec les ongles chargés de caractères qu'il traçoit dessus avec une épingle : ces caractères lui remettoient dans l'esprit diverses pensées qui auroient pu lui échapper, en sorte que ce grand homme revenoit chez lui comme une abeille chargée de miel."

[2] Henri Poincaré, *Science and Method*, tr. Francis Maitland (Nelson, 1914), p. 53 : " I left Caen, where I was then living, to take part in a geological conference arranged by the School of Mines. The incidents of the journey made me forget my mathematical work. When we got to Coutances we got into a break to go for a drive, and, just as I put my foot on the step, the idea came to me, though nothing in my former thoughts seemed to have prepared me for it, that the transformations I had used to define Fuchsian functions were identical with those of non-Euclidean geometry. . . ."
" I then began to study arithmetical questions without any great apparent result, and without suspecting that they could have the least connexion with my previous researches. Disgusted at my want of success, I went away to spend a few days at the seaside, and thought of entirely different things. One day, as I was walking on the cliff, the idea came to me, again with the same characteristics of conciseness, suddenness, and immediate certainty, that arithmetical transformations of indefinite ternary quadratic forms are identical with those of non-Euclidian geometry."
He returned to Caen and worked out with conscious effort all that was involved in this result.

afternoon walk, thinking of nothing in particular, there would flow into his mind, with sudden and unaccountable emotion, sometimes a line or two or verse, sometimes a whole stanza at once, accompanied and not preceded by a vague outline of the poem of which they were destined to form part. Then there would usually be a lull for an hour or so; and then the spring would " bubble up again ". " When I got home ", he continues, " I wrote them down, leaving gaps and hoping that further inspiration might be forthcoming some other day. . . . Sometimes the poem had to be taken in hand and completed by the brain, which was apt to be a matter of trouble and anxiety, involving trial and disappointment and sometimes ending in failure." [1] Unlike Browning's wise thrush, he could not recapture " that first fine careless rapture ", but who can tell how much trouble he might have saved himself if he had followed the advice of the White Queen and had at once " made a memorandum of it ",[2] and not waited till he had reached home?

Joubert was wiser. " In bed or up and about," M. P. de Raynal tells us,

" in his study or while he took his walks, afoot or in his carriage, he always had with him a little gold pencil (fountain-pens were not as yet) and his little note-book, and his impressions were committed to it with a constancy which never failed him (qui ne se démentjamais), but without arrangement (suite), without fuss, and with complete indifference as to whether any one saw him ".[3]

Such examples of how the human mind works and how wise men deal with, and meet, its capriciousness might be multiplied indefinitely, but they are summed up in Captain Cuttle's advice, " When found, make a note of," [4] with the additional precept, " Always carry about a note-book with you."

---

[1] *The Name and Nature of Poetry* (Cambridge, 1933), p. 49.
[2] Lewis Carroll, *Through the Looking-Glass*, Ch. I, p. 19:
" 'The horror of that moment', the King went on, ' I shall never, never forget.'
" 'You will, though,' said the Queen, 'if you don't make a memorandum of it.' "
[3] *Pensées*, Vol. I (Paris, 1884), *La Vie et les Travaux de M. J. Joubert*, p. lxxxix.
[4] Dickens, *Dombey and Son*, Ch. XV: " 'Wal'r my boy,' replied the captain, ' in the Proverbs of Solomon you will find the following words, " May we never want a friend in need nor a bottle to give him ! When found, make a note of." ' Here the captain stretched out his hand to Walter, with an air of right good faith that spoke volumes; at the same time repeating (for he felt proud of the accuracy of his quotation), " 'When found, make a note of'."

A second precept is called for at once. Enter each note on a separate sheet. This is a general principle in business correspondence. If several different matters have to be dealt with in one letter, each should be easily detachable, so that it may be sent to the department or employee that has to attend to it. This will save an immense amount of time and trouble.

It is also a general principle of study and of using the results of study, as, for instance, in the writing of history. "Most beginners", says M. Victor Langlois,

" who are not warned beforehand . . . keep . . . note-books which they fill continuously and progressively with notes on the texts they are interested in. This method is utterly wrong. The materials collected must be classified sooner or later; otherwise it would be necessary, when occasion arose, to deal separately with the materials bearing on a given point, to read right through the whole series of note-books, and this laborious process would have to be repeated every time a new detail was wanted. If this method seems attractive at first, it is because it appears to save time. But this is false economy; the ultimate result is an enormous addition to the labour of search, and a great difficulty in combining the materials." [1]

It is the necessary method for any lexicographer, who by it becomes less of the " harmless drudge " that Dr. Johnson wrote him down. The compiling of the great *Oxford English Dictionary* was possible only by the adoption from the beginning of an elaborate system of cards—separate slips for each word and quotation. " By the directions ", the Editors write in their *Introduction*,

" which were issued to the intending readers in 1858, uniformity in the method of presenting the quotations was attained. Each was written on a separate slip of paper, at first of the size of a half-sheet of note-paper, latterly on a quarter of a sheet of foolscap, except when readers who supplied their own paper . . . wrote

[1] *Introduction to the Study of History,* by Ch. V. Langlois and Ch. Seignobos, tr. G. C. Berry (Duckworth, 1898), Bk. II, Ch. iv, p. 103. He continues: " Everyone admits nowadays that it is advisable to collect materials on separate cards or slips of paper. The notes from each document are entered upon a loose leaf furnished with the precisest possible indications of origin. The advantages of this artifice are obvious: the detachability of the slips enables us to group them at will in a host of different combinations ; if necessary, to change their places : it is easy to bring texts of the same kind together, and to incorporate additions, as they are required, in the interior of the groups to which they belong."

on pieces of any size or quality that came to hand. . . . When completed, the normal slip presented three things (1) the word for which it was selected, (2) the date, author, title page, etc., of the work cited, and (3) the quotation itself, either in full, or in an adequate form." [1]

So do not use a " Reporter's " note-book for these ideas that suddenly come. Keep it for things that have to be reported continuously by date, for diaries, notes of minutes, of lessons given day in day out, of lectures taken down once a week. Even so there is always a danger that you will find you have brought the wrong book, and odd, confusing cross-references will have to be inserted. I well remember the trouble I gave myself when I was gathering the material for my *Baptism and Christian Archaeology*.[2] I entered my findings in one of these " Reporter's " note-books, and the number of times I had to turn its pages backwards and forwards, and the confusing necessity of marking notes as having been transcribed and incorporated into the text, taught me a lesson.

Avoid, too, the snare of Commonplace Books. They are generally too large to be carried about. Like Mary Bennett, you are tempted to make extracts that are not worth making. You can get rid of them only by tearing out a page, even if you keep to the rule of a separate page for each entry. Entries that you want get buried, and can be found only if you keep up an elaborate system of cross-references and indexing . . . which probably you will not do.

Therefore *always carry about with you* not merely a note-book, but *a " tablet " or " tab " note-book—that is, one with perforated and detachable leaves.*[3]

Enter everything with full references. It will save trouble in the long run. If you merely enter the surname of the author whom you quote, without his initials, you may have to look through many pages in the library catalogue when you want to verify your reference and

---

[1] *A New English Dictionary on Historical Principles.* Introduction, Supplement and Bibliography (Oxford, 1933), p. xiv.
[2] *Studia Biblica*, Vol. V, Part iv (Oxford University Press, 1903).
[3] Langlois and Seignobos, *op. cit.*, p. 104: " The method of slips is not without its drawbacks. Each slip ought to be furnished with precise references to the source from which its contents have been derived; consequently, if a document has been analysed upon fifty different slips, the same reference must be repeated fifty times. Hence a slight increase in the amount of writing to be done. It is certainly on account of this trivial complication that some obstinately cling to the inferior note-book system ".

read your quotation again in its original context. There are many volumes by "Smith" in the British Museum Catalogue. Always enter the date of publication and the edition quoted. It is not that facts alter or that good work ever gets out of date, but new facts may arise or be discovered, and you want to know if anything else has been done or said since your author wrote. Take down, too, the name of the publisher, or at least the place of publication. You may want to order the book at a shop, and the entry will help the bookseller to trace it. See that you enter a sufficient (and accurate) title, the volume and the page, as well as, in most cases, the chapter and verse of the whole work. If your quotation exceeds the page of your " tab " note-book, number the second and following pages, add a short reference to the author, and clip the pages together directly after tearing them out.

Fix your own symbols and abbreviations. Exact quotations should be enclosed in inverted commas, your summary or notes of a passage written without. Your own comments and ideas that may occur to you in taking notes may be put in brackets. Words underlined are understood by printers to be set up in italics, so keep underlining for the author's italic words in quotation or for words that you would wish to be so set up if you were going to have your writing printed. Mark passages that you wish to be able to refer to again without difficulty by a line at the side, or by two lines if they seem to you to be specially important. Doubt may be expressed by a query in brackets " (?)," definite disagreement by a note of exclamation " (!) ", or, as Mr. Gladstone did, by writing in the Italian for " but "—" ma ". Fix on some mark to show that you have checked a reference. If you use the same symbol to signify that you have made use of it, add a short indication where you have done so—e.g., Serm. Oct. 15. '42. Words may be contracted—e.g., " w." for " with ", " agst." for " against ". Symbols may be used for names. It is not irreverent to write " X " for " Christ ", or " Xian " for " Christian ", but be careful that you do not make too many symbols and abbreviations and forget what they stand for.

Write each entry under a heading, if possible in three words. These may be underlined twice to catch the eye. This will keep you to the point and do much to prevent your making long extracts merely because a passage seems to you well expressed, though about nothing in particular. In short, (1) *always carry about with you a note-book*, (2) *enter everything on a separate page*, (3) *and let the note-book be a " tablet " note-book*. This was the advice I repeated to my class till the bare mention of a " tab note-book " provoked a laugh. Then I knew that at last I had got my advice home.[1]

II

Next for the sorting of your material. You should separate the entries that may help you in future sermons from such things as postal addresses, notes of visits, lists of things to do, titles of books, etc. The ideas that come to you in the way we have examined above are those that interest you, that you have made your own, even if they are not original.

" Nothing ", wrote Keats, " ever becomes real till it is experienced. . . . Even a proverb is no proverb till your life has illustrated it."[2]

If they have interested you, they will, or at least may, interest others. *Si vis me flere prius dolendum est* [3] involves a principle that

[1] The entries in mine when I was putting together what I have written above were as follows:

(1) A draft letter on the South India Church Reunion scheme.
(2) A rough outline for a sermon on " Custom and Habit ".
(3) A note on the essential evil of fox-hunting—that it gives rein to the instinct to kill while preventing the huntsman from realising it by the distractions of horse and hound.
(4) A quotation from Aristotle's *Ethics* on regarding things rather than persons as good or true.
(5) A note on the Tractarians and Social Work from a book of Miss Yonge's.
(6) A reference that still needed to be checked.
(7) A quotation from the Abbé Calvet on Montaigne.
(8) One from Aristotle on the meaning of " Bourgeois ".
(9) Aquinas on Isaiah 45. 7, " I create evil ".
(10) Dowden on *Kyrie Eleison* as not the work of a committee.
(11) An address to be entered in my address book.
(12) Plotinus on the world as rational..
(13) Logic and the impossibility of knowing what does not exist.
(14) Note on Mrs. Eddy and her " Logical Conversion ".

[2] *The Letters of John Keats,* ed. M. B. Farmer (Oxford, 1941), Fri., March 19, p. 423.

[3] Horace, *Ars Poetica,* v. 102, " If you want me to weep you must grieve first yourself."

Cp. Goethe, *Faust,* tr. G. M. Cookson. Routledge's Broadway Translation (1929),

> " Wenn ihr's nicht fühlt, ihr werdet's nicht erjagen,
> Wenn es nicht aus der Seele dringt,
> Und mit urkräftigem Behagen
> Die Herzen aller Hörer zwingt.
>
> .   .   .   .
>
> Doch werdet ihr nie Herz zu Herzen schaffen
> Wenn es euch nicht von Herzen geht."

But the feeling must have been there long before the preacher has got into the pulpit.

applies to interest as much as to emotion. To rouse interest in others does more than exhortation. Besides, there is something unseemly, especially in the young preacher, in exhortation, by the inexperienced, of those who are both older in years and more tried in the knowledge of life. But there is always a great temptation, from the mere fact of being in a pulpit, to fall back on appeal. Besides, it demands so much less trouble, though it is difficult to steer a course between patronising and apologising: whereas the youngest preacher who speaks with the student's right to speak on what he has studied can do so without offence.

Again, his ideas will be new ideas, if only in their application and setting. " Let no one say," wrote Pascal in one of his *Thoughts*, " that what I say is not new. The matter is newly put." [1] It was new because it just expressed what he wanted to say on the particular subject in hand in the exact way he wanted to say it.

So with quotations. They can easily be overdone. Some authors have read so widely that they seem to think in quotations and become very tiresome to read. It sounds a conceited thing to say, but a thing said in your own words is generally better said for the purpose in view than the same thing said by a classic author. A sermon made up of quotations from the Bible (such as was once presented to me by a student) is not a good sermon. But, on the other hand, a thing is better taken in if said several times over. The secret of oratory, it has been said, is to say the same thing over and over again, in different words if you can, in the same if you cannot.

But when you have said a thing clearly it is useful to say it again in better words than your own. When you have made your meaning plain it is useful to show that it is not only your opinion, that it has been said by others whose words carry a greater weight of authority than do yours. If you can support your contention by a relevant quotation from one who knows, you have done much to establish your point. A quotation at the close of a period or at the end of a paragraph has a great power to bring about understanding and conviction. A book which puts its case clearly in the text and supports its contentions with *pièces justificatives* and suggestions for further reading in notes at the bottom of the page, is often the best value for money, the book you want to buy and keep.

Similarly with illustrations. They, too, enable us to say a thing again in the words of others. They may, of course, be made a substitute for thought:—

[1] *Pensées*, ed. Brunschvicg, No. 22: " Qu'on ne dise pas que je n'ai rien dit de nouveau: la disposition des matières est nouvelle."

" Denn eben wo Begriffe fehlen
Da stellt ein Wort zur rechten Zeit sich ein." [1]

(said Mephistopheles, posing as Dr. Faust to the inquiring student who thought of reading theology), and a Dictionary of Quotations should be used only to check passages that have stuck in reading; but, rightly chosen, they reinforce what has been said by saying it again in better words and as part of a larger view. They often, too, bring the required emotion that produces memory and conviction, in language which the young preacher has not yet acquired the right to use, but which he may rightly borrow from a larger experience than his own.

Stories are understood and remembered—and that not only by simple people—where arguments are not followed and advice is forgotten. "Truth embodied in a tale", Tennyson has reminded us, " may enter in at lowly doors," and we have good authority for teaching by parables. But stories noted in reading must nearly always be rewritten in the preacher's own words. To repeat them in full takes too much time, for the eye reads more quickly than the tongue speaks, and, at best, leaves them looming too large in the hearer's recollection. Everything unessential to the point should be cut out. They can hardly be made too short. Mere allusions are, no doubt, worse than useless to all but the very well read, but if a pruned story be told slowly, much of what has been cut out will be suggested to, and be supplied by, the congregation for themselves.

But the great thing is that right ideas, apt quotations, relevant illustrations, and telling stories, must be *noted and collected beforehand*.

III

What is to be done with the material as it accumulates? How is it to be filed and stored?

When once a thing has been secured in the " tab " note-book it is there. You can go through the entries at your convenience, and sort them where you can be sure of finding them again. Some can be dealt with there and then. Notes made of things to be done can be torn up when you have done them and the necessary report or entry has been made in the proper place. Addresses when entered in your address book or diary need not be kept any longer. Visits to be paid, a list of letters to be answered, a programme of work for

---

[1] " For there precisely where ideas fail a word comes opportunely into play."

the day, need not be kept when a fresh list of things still to be done has been made out.

There remain, then, notes of ideas. Some of these are obviously futile. They struck you at the time you made them, but second thoughts show that they are not worth keeping, so tear them out. Others, though of more worth, remain obstinately unattached and single. No other entries under the same heading have been made; they have not attracted to themselves any other ideas. Some are analyses or notes of books you have been reading or, more probably, a few disconnected notes made as you read them in an easy-chair. If the book is your own you may file these in the book itself, though if there are several pages of such notes they do not improve the binding of the book. It is difficult to know what should be done with other such entries. Some may be filed in a " concertina " file, but experience shows that they generally get buried there. Or they may be put together in a large envelope, and gone through again at intervals. So, too, with those entries you do not tear out because you " might want them some time ". Before long there will be a number of eviscerated old note-books, each containing three or four entries you did not like to destroy. But they will probably have to rest in peace till your executors burn them.

Complete analyses of books are different, but these should have been made on larger sheets which can be clipped together and filed in alphabetical order under the authors' names, and with their exact titles, or according to their subject. They can be treated practically as the books themselves would be if the reader had them. A very fair working library can be built up in this way by a reader who cannot afford to buy many books or has little space in which to store them, at any rate till he is settled in a house. It is a fairly safe rule to follow never to buy any book till you have read it and know that you will want to refer to it again. Reference or " Dictionary " books are those to which the poor student should confine himself. The others he should get from libraries, and make from them notes of things he thinks he may want in the future.

There remain the entries in the note-book made for use in sermons the subjects of which have already been thought of. Those with the same headings should be clipped together, or put in an envelope with the title outside. These can be kept in a cardboard box with a list of the subjects on the top. Some will hang fire, but most will slowly add to their numbers. Of others it will soon be found that you have enough material for the middle chief part of some sermon; of many that you have more than enough, so that

you can select what are most to the point, while the rest remain as a
nucleus for a second sermon later on to carry on the subject. After
the sermon has been preached such additional notes may be filed
in the MS. of the sermon itself with a view to future use or a recasting
of what has been preached.

We are now thinking chiefly of the mechanism of sermon-
writing, but such is the basis of all literary or lecturing work. For
some years I made a note or extract from anything I came across in
which writers or speakers said that " things are not what they used
to be ", or that " religion was rapidly dying out ", and filed them
under the title *Good Old Times*. The quotations accumulated, each
with its author and date, till on looking them through and sorting
them by decades and centuries and periods I found I had enough
references to every ten years of the last three centuries, from nearly
every century of the Middle Ages, and examples from the ancient
world both after and before the Christian Era which seems to prove
that things had been growing worse and worse ever since the Flood.
Which is absurd, as Euclid used to say. It was no trouble to write
an article on the subject; the work had nearly all been done
before.[1]

So to make up a lecture and to write it out demands little labour
at the time of writing if you know your subject—that is, if years
before you have read steadily about it and taken notes of what you
thought really mattered. To write a book takes time. You have
to fix your subject, to search out with attention what is relevant to it,
to impregnate your mind with it, and to be continually on the alert
to note the thoughts that seem to rise spontaneously about it, to try
out parts of it in speech or discussion, to cut out irrelevances in the
plan and to verify references till there comes that unmistakable
feeling that you really know it. The preparing for the printer,
reading proofs, making an index are tedious tasks, but the actual
writing, which matters most, is the least part of the labour of composition if the preliminary steps have been duly taken.

There is an exasperatingly silly story, repeated *ad nauseam* in
books on homiletics, about how a young student just ordained
asked his bishop for advice about preaching, who, it is said, replied,
" Some men prepare their sermons "; and then, after an impressive
pause, or at least one meant to be impressive, added, " Others
prepare themselves ", and sent the poor young man away either
with the impression that if you are good you need not take any

<hr>

[1] *The Quarterly Review*, October, 1940. See below, page 61.

trouble with your work, or that the bishop had nothing helpful to tell him as to how he was to train himself for his special calling. I hope at least that I have been more practically helpful in suggesting that the *first step is to read steadily and widely in order to secure those thoughts that seem to come of themselves, and become your own, as a result,* and that *the way to do so is always to carry about with you a " tab " note-book.*

II

THE PSYCHOLOGY OF THOUGHT

THE COMPOSITION OF THE SERMON

" As the Pythagoreans say, the world and all that is in it is determined by the number three, since beginning, and middle, and end give the number of an ' all ', and the number they give is the triad. And so having taken these three from Nature as (so to speak) laws of it, we make further use of it in the worship of the Gods. . . . And in this as we have said, we do but follow the lead which Nature gives."—Aristotle, *De Coelo*, I, 1, 268a12, tr. J. L. Stocks.

" Avant donc que d'écrire, apprenez à penser :
  Selon que nôtre idée est plus ou moins obscure,
  L'expression la suit, ou moins nette, ou plus pure ;
  Ce que l'on conçoit bien s'énonce clairement,
  Et les mots pour le dire arrivent aisément."
        —Boileau, *L'Art Poétique*, Chant I, l. 150.

" Learn then to Think ere you pretend to Write,
  As are our Sentiments Obscure or Clear,
  So will our Diction Bright or Dull Appear,
  What we conceive, with Ease we can express ;
  Words to the Notions flow with Readiness."
    —The Works of Monsieur Boileau made English from the last Paris edition, by Several hands. To which is prefixed HIS LIFE written by JOSEPH ADDISON Esq. by Mr. Des Maizeaux. And some account of this translation by N. Rowe Esq. Adorned with Cuts. Vol. I (London, 1712), p. 91.

" What shall I say first? what next? what last of all? "
        —Homer, *Odyssey*, IX, 14.

WHEN the preacher has collected his material and has a good store of these " fringe thoughts " which are his own, how is he to " get it over " to his congregation? How do they think? How do all men think? What are some of the chief elements of the universal laws of human thought that are relevant to his task?

Certain of them may be discovered by a simple experiment. Let a lecturer ask his class, " What was my last lecture about? " and note the immediate reaction to his question. Or better, let him ask what the last lecture of one of his colleagues was about, to avoid stressing the memory of things seen overmuch by his presence. Sight memory is always the strongest, and the majority will show this by their eyes in one way or another. Some will shut them to

18

prevent objects present distracting the recollection of what they saw in the other room, and they will probably draw back their heads a little. Others will fix their eyes but look at nothing. Possibly they will put their hands to their foreheads; almost certainly they will frown. Their object in doing so is to shut out sights and recall what they heard. They will hear again striking sentences as the tones and modulations of his voice ring in their ears. Others, again, will automatically look down at their desks, and perhaps move their fingers along them; they are trying to see again what they heard and wrote down in their own words in their notes, and these are the ones who will remember most vividly and accurately, because it is not mere passive impressions that they revive, but mental activity of their own.

For in most thought there are three elements. There are things that we see. Animals, it would seem, get little beyond visual imagery. A dog apparently will dream and see again what it saw when awake, but it is doubtful whether it can recall even sights at will, and almost certain that it cannot reason.[1] There are sounds, too, that we heard and remember by repetition, that we associate with things seen, and so give names to—the prerogative of Adam. But only when the association of sight and sound is joined to the activities of tongue and lips in the form of speech, with its phrases and sentences, and only fully when we have learned to do this silently without actual motion in the mouth and to express them in movements of the hand in writing, can we be said really to think, remember, and reason.[2]

These different activities of the mind are connected with move-ments of different centres of the brain. That of sight lies farthest back; that of hearing more in the centre but lower down; that of

[1] Aristotle, *Politics*, I, i, 10, 1253a : " For Nature, as we declare, does nothing without purpose, and man alone of animals possesses speech. The mere voice, it is true, can indicate pain or pleasure, and therefore is pos-sessed by animals as well—but speech is designed to indicate the advantageous and the harmful, and therefore is the special privilege of man in distinction from the other animals that he alone has perception of good and bad and right and wrong and the other moral qualities."

[2] Cp. Antoine Rivarol, *Discours sur l'universalité de la langue Française* (Paris, Delagrave, 1929), p. 57: " Si la parole est une pensée qui manifeste, il faut que la pensée soit une parole interieure et cachée. L'homme qui parle est donc l'homme qui pense tout haut : et si on peut juger un homme par ses paroles, on peut aussi juger une nation par son langage." (If speech is a thought which reveals itself then thought is an inner speech that hides itself. The man who speaks is therefore the man who thinks aloud, and if we can judge a man by his words we can also judge a nation by its mother tongue.)

C

motion of the organs of speech in a position in front; that of motions of the hand in writing in the middle of the brain, but above that of hearing. They are connected, suggests William James, by brain-paths which help to unify the impressions as coherent thoughts, and facilitate the repetition of the combined motions in memory and understanding.[1] Details of the physical theory may be criticised, but at least it corresponds to the facts of our experience.

The use of the eyes comes first in time, but in both speech and writing, when developed as arts, we are apt to forget the importance of sight in clear thought and of sound in pleasing diction, and to rely on our silent thinking and the look of the printed word. So sermons often lack lucidity, for the people do not see what the preacher means. There is no pattern, no variety. The sermons fail also to command attention, for they do not appeal to the ear, and in consequence fail to interest, to persuade, or to convince. They become a mere sequence of words and thoughts with no coherence or rhythm. "The man of eloquence", wrote Cicero from his experience in the law courts of Rome (and Augustine borrowed his idea in lecturing to the clergy of Africa),

" will be one who is able to speak in court, or in deliberative bodies so as to prove, to please, and to persuade. To prove is the first necessity; to please is to charm; to sway is victory; for it is the one thing of all that avails most in winning verdicts."[2]

"Style", wrote Buffon, "lies in the balance and sequence of ideas rather than in the harmony of sound."[3] So Rule Number One in homilectics is, *First see your sermon.*

[1] Cp. William James, *The Principles of Psychology* (Macmillan, 1890), Vol. I, p. 56: "There is no ' centre of speech ' in the brain any more than there is a faculty of speech in the mind. The entire brain, more or less, is at work in a man who uses language." He illustrates this by a diagram.

[2] *Orator*, XX, 69. Quoted, with a slight alteration, by Augustine, *De Doctrina Christiana*, IV, 12, 27: "Est igitur eloquens qui ita dicet ut probat, ut delectet, ut flectat . . . probare, necessitatis est; delectare, suavitatis, flectere, victoriae."

[3] *Discourse pronounced at the French Academy on the Day of his Reception as a member in* 1753. He adds: "If you connect them (thoughts) straitly, if you link them together (what you write) becomes firm, nervous, and concise. If you let them just follow one another, and only connect them by the help of words, however choice they may be, the style will be diffuse, slack and trailing." Quoted by Sainte Beuve, *Port Royal* (Hachette, 1860), Vol. II, p. 327.

Cp. De Saci. "On oublie que la veritable éloquence est dans les choses, et non dans les expressions. On estime bien plus un peintre qui a dessin que celui qui n'a que le maniement d'un pinceau." (We forget that true eloquence lies in things and not in phrases. We think much more of a painter who has composition than of one who has merely dexterity with his brush.)

I

The sermon should have a shape. Things in a pattern are easier to see and therefore easier to understand and to remember. What makes a pattern?

A pattern implies proportion and balance in its different parts. The parts may be of different sizes, but one thing should not take up all the room. There should be balance of ideas. The more important should loom larger, but their very importance is thrown into relief by lesser adjuncts. The whole should have order. One thing should lead to another, while all should be in the line that leads to the point.[1] This saves effort and avoids confusion, since it is easier to follow what is naturally connected with what you are thinking about, while it is distracting to go off into side issues, and exhausting to be continually jumping from one thing to another, however interesting each may be in itself. A pattern should have variety. Change and contrast make things easier to picture, where monotony is fatiguing and exasperating. The continued jerking of a single bell before a service does not produce an attitude of devotion or receptivity.

Pattern and plan make for lucidity in a sermon. The word " lucidity " is based on a metaphor drawn from sight. The art of window-dressing lies in making a harmonious composition of the things you have for sale. The title-page of a book, by the use of different types, tells you the character of the pages that follow and invites you to read. In advertisements on hoardings or in the newspaper the art of the printer to make people notice lies in " displaying " his matter by pictures, by variety of type, above all by beginning lines at different distances from the margin, or " insetting ". In handwriting and manuscript we are limited to insetting and underlining, and, only in a very limited degree, to variation of current script and block letters. So the first step is to see your sermon and *make an outline*.

Do your main work here. When once you have begun to write it is difficult to alter anything without destroying the balance of what has already been written. In the outline it is easy to add illustrations or quotations. You can transpose one part to another

---

[1] A sermon will thus have " that architectural conception of work which foresees the end in the beginning and never loses sight of it and in every part is conscious of all the rest, till the last sentence does, but with undiminished vigour, unfold and justify the first—a condition of literary art, which, in contradistinction to another quality of the artist himself to be spoken of later, I shall call ' mind in style '."—Walter Pater, *Appreciations, with an essay on Style* (Macmillan, 1893), p. 18.

en bloc if you see that the order is wrong and that the less important
follows the more and forms an anti-climax.   Moreover, it is easier
to see what is really irrelevant and should be cut out altogether.
There will then be no need to follow Dr. Johnson's useful but painful
advice to " read over your compositions, and wherever you meet with
a passage which you think is particularly fine, strike it out ".[1]

A thing as a whole is usually improved by cutting out what is not
really needed.   It is said that Phil May got his power of directness
and suggestion in the few lines of his drawings in *Punch* by first
making a full and elaborate picture and then cutting out every line
that was not absolutely essential to his conception.   So the student
should first train himself in terseness of expression.   In reading a
book he should learn to sum up in the fewest possible words the idea
or ideas of each paragraph.   He should practise himself in thus
analysing its contents as if he were preparing to add marginals in a
new edition.   We all know how it helps when books are printed
with such headings.   He should learn how to sum up the main
ideas each in a separate line, and if there are subordinate ideas they
should be inset a little to the right in his notes.   Of course he need
not do this for every book that he reads.   He will soon find out that
some are not worth the trouble, but he should always have one or
two in hand that he is analysing.   In this way he will not only get
a manuscript library of notes of books he cannot afford to buy, but
will learn to see, and think clearly, in outline.   In the same way he
should keep up his habit, begun (I hope) in attending classes at
College, of taking notes of lectures or sermons he hears, not necessarily keeping them, but for continual practice in summing up in his
own words what he hears from another.

Sometimes he will find that the paragraph forms no pattern and
has no particular leading idea.   He will then realise why it failed to
interest him or seemed so difficult to understand.[2]   At others he
will find that a passage is so packed with thought that he cannot

---

[1] Boswell's *Life* (Oxford Edition), Vol. II, p. 237, April 30, 1773.
[2] Cp. P. J. Hartog, *The Writing of English* (Oxford, 1907), p. 66.   The
writer, after speaking of the value of analysis and précis-writing, says:
" The first aim of the exercise is obviously to reveal the plan, conscious or
unconscious, of the author.   On one occasion my class, who were as it so
happened, nearly all Radicals, had, they told me, listened with great delight
to the speech of a distinguished Liberal leader, and I suggested to them to
summarise the first two columns of his speech as reported in the *Manchester
Guardian*.   They came back next week with the unexpected but unanimous
verdict, made plain by their summaries, that the speech was ' badly composed '.   I comforted them with the suggestion that a speech may sometimes
be ' composed ' to meet the changing moods of a volatile audience, and

shorten it, but will see how the ideas in it follow in sequence and balance one another.

Take, for example, the opening words of Hooker's *Ecclesiastical Polity*—a passage we used to choose as a penultimate test in the elocution competition for the reading prize at King's College.

" He that goeth about to persuade a multitude, that they are not so well governed as they ought to be, shall never want attentive and favourable hearers; because they know the manifold defects whereunto every kind of regiment is subject, but the secret lets and difficulties, which in public proceedings are innumerable and inevitable, they have not ordinarily the judgment to consider. And because such as openly reprove supposed disorders of state are taken for principal friends to the common benefit of all, and for men that carry singular freedom of mind; under this fair and plausible colour whatsoever they utter passeth for good and current. That which wanteth in the weight of their speech, is supplied by the aptness of men's minds to accept and believe it. Whereas on the other side, if we maintain things that are established, we have not only to strive with a number of heavy prejudices deeply rooted in the hearts of men, who think that herein we serve the time, and speak in favour of the present state, because thereby we either hold or seek preferment; but also to bear such exceptions as minds so averted beforehand usually take against that which they are loth should be poured into them."

Hardly a word can be spared in analysis, but it may be noted down in this form :—

The would-be reformer
    always gets a good audience.
        Men know what is wrong,
            but don't know the difficulties.
Critics taken to be friends,
    and open-minded;
        So arguments seem good,
            even if poor are readily accepted.

---

assured them that the distinguished orator in question would certainly not republish his speech as he had delivered it to the damage of his literary reputation. But their verdict showed conclusively that the members of the class were no longer content to submit their judgment to a popular opinion, or to their own first impressions."

As a further exercise the Table of Contents of this book might be compared with the text as written out.

Whereas
    Conservatives assumed biassed,
      " Time-serving " and " On the make ",
        Apart from natural aversion to change.

It will be seen that it falls into a pattern of three parts; the first stating the problem, and the next two balancing the claims of the two rival solvers, while each section is made clear in three or four steps. As Mark Pattison said [1]:—

> " Hooker's elaborate sentence, like the sentence of Demos-thenes, is composed of parts so hinged, of clauses so subordinated to the main thought, that we foresee the end from the beginning, and close the period with a sense of perfect roundness and totality."

II

What is the pattern of the sermon to be? This depends on certain principles underlying the nature of sight and its relation to human understanding.

If I take a handful of coins and throw down in turn two, three, or even four on the table, you will be able to tell at once how many they are. But when I throw one more there is a little hesitation. The eye groups them into two, $3 + 2$ or $4 + 1$, and does a very rapid addition sum to realise that there are five. So you will notice that churchwardens counting the collection will separate shillings and sixpences with three fingers of the right hand before arranging them in piles. Bankers will do the same in counting out five shillings' worth of coppers, though sometimes they will use two fingers of each hand and count by fours. Even with continuous daily practice they still find this the easiest and surest way.

If you look round any ordinary old-fashioned room you will see at once if there are three panes from left to right in the window and four from top to bottom, and so by a rapid calculation that there are twelve in all; but you have to calculate. As I write in a quasi-Gothic library, I see at once that there are four panes across and four up to a transom, and that above it there are two rows of four each, but I have to multiply $4 \times 4 = 16$ to know that there are sixteen below, and $2 \times 4 = 8$ to realise that there are eight in the upper part. The next window is twice the size, but I cannot see at a glance how

---

[1] *Milton*, " English Men of Letters " Series (Macmillan, 1879), p. 70.

many panes there are across it. I have to see it as two windows divided by a slightly heavier mullion.

On the shelf in front of me I see directly that there are four volumes of the *Encyclopaedia Biblica*. I see fairly quickly that there are five of Hastings' *Dictionary of the Bible*, but that is because there are three on one shelf and two on another. I see this by looking at them, and the addition sum $2 + 3 = 5$ is almost spontaneous, though not quite. There are twelve of the *Schaff-Herzog Encyclopedia*, but, to count them, the quickest way is to divide them up into sets of three and do the sum. All I can say offhand about Hastings' *Encyclopaedia of Religion and Ethics* is that there are a good number of volumes. Exactly how many is found out most easily and quickly by getting up and looking at the number of the last volume of " Indices, etc., etc."

This power of direct recognition of numbers can be extended by formal arrangement. In playing cards immediate recognition of the number of pips on each is required. From the ace to four there is no difficulty. The five has to be in a conventional form of four in a square with one in the middle. The six has to be two sets of three side by side. The seven starts a new third column in the middle. For nine, side-columns of four have to be employed. But for numbers above ten you could not use side columns of five; you would always have to be looking to see if they were of four or five. It is easier, therefore, as you want three more cards, to fall back on pictures of knave, queen, and king. You might use a middle column of four and so get cards up to sixteen, but the recognition of four is not quite so quick as that of three, and confusion would arise.

The same principle guides the form of Roman numerals. They are still used on our watch and clock dials. We can recognise the numbers up to four easily. But we could not distinguish IIII from IIIII at once except from its position. Therefore a new letter has to be called into use for 5—namely, V—and IV for 4 is more easily recognised at once than IIII.

This " rule of three " extends to all objects of sight. If you look at pictures you will see that good artists generally make a pattern of three (or four) chief objects and another of three (or four) highest lights. If you cover up one, the picture seems to fall to pieces. The amateur photographer, as long as he merely takes snapshots, invariably finds that his prints are improved by cutting down till there are three (or four) chief objects left. A photograph of a College group may be an interesting reminder of companionship in bygone days, but it is an ugly object on the wall, while Rembrandt

could make a group of six Dutch Syndics into a fine picture.[1] This
is what in Art we call composition.

But sight as an element of thought is, as we saw, closely connected with hearing, and in sound the same law obtains. In
rhythm, two-, three- or four-time is easy to listen to and to conduct.
Six-time is heard as two sets of three notes. Five- or seven-time is
sometimes used, but five-time becomes made up of four beats with
an extra one to throw out the rhythm and prevent its becoming
heavy, and the rhythm of seven-time is beaten as alternate bars of
three and four. So, too, in harmony the common chord, major or
minor, is naturally recognised because it has three notes (or four if the
key note is doubled in the octave), and that of the dominant seventh,
with its four, is easily taken in; but chords with more notes have to
be learned to be recognised, as had the higher values of playing-cards.

The same law applies to verse. The simplest poems and those
easiest to understand are in verses of three or four lines. Most
ballads, psalm translations, narrative poems, and hymns are in
common measure. Where songs (as lyrics) are intended to be sung,
or of a type originally meant for music, the verses are generally
more elaborate, but are still built up of sets of twos, threes, and fours.
The sonnet is perhaps the classic example of such structure with its
two sets of four lines followed by two sets of three or, in the Shake-
spearian form, with three sets of four lines followed by a couplet as
the fourth part. If anything is attempted beyond this the poem
becomes not a lyric but an ode in which, as in the epic, it is the sense
of sustained narration that is called forth.

So, too, songs are generally of three verses. In the Victorian
ballad the principle ran wild. The first two verses were in the major
and the third in the minor when hopes were dashed and the tragedy
complete, or the first two, in which the little maiden and her flowers
were lost in the snow, were followed by a third in which she ascended
with angels to heaven to the accompaniment of chords in triplets
played on the top notes of the piano.[2] In the Handelian air the

---

[1] Take, for instance, the well-known picture by De Hooch in the
National Gallery, which presents an ordinary picture of a Dutch courtyard
with two women and a child standing in it. In the left-hand bottom corner
there is a bucket which seems to play no particular part in the scene. But
cover it up with your hand and the whole balance of the picture is destroyed.

[2] *The Times* for August 20, 1941, quoted the following lines by Owen
Seaman on the structure of the Victorian Royalty Ballad.

> "See that the verses are few, darling!
> Keep to the rule of three,
> That will be better for you, darling!
> Certainly better for me."

Rembrandt: The Syndics, Amsterdam.

The Parson Preaching

P. de Hooch: A Dutch Courtyard, National Gallery, London.

Facing page 27

subject was answered by the counter-subject and completed by a repetition of the first theme. The same principles appear in dances grouped in sets of three forming the basis of the suite and ultimately the groundwork of the sonata with its first movement of subject and counter-subject, its slow movement, and its final quick movement.

The Welsh are singers and poets by nature, and their national character comes out in their hymnody. A glance through a Welsh hymn-book will reveal, even to anyone quite unfamiliar with their language, the richness and variety of their metres. A certain few, no doubt, are of four-line verses, but the great majority of stanzas are combinations of groups of three or four lines. The tunes themselves are generally formed of three parts—a phrase sung and repeated, a counter-phrase, and a final repetition of the first. Moreover, it will be noticed that the hymns themselves are very rarely of four verses; generally they are of three or only two, unless they are in common metre. Of the four-verse hymns, generally only two or perhaps only one verse is sung. If that is felt to be insufficient the last half of the verse is repeated, often more than once.

Now, we have all sung "Through the night of doubt and sorrow", and have felt it heavy. It drags along through eight four-line verses. The over-emphasis of the popular tune, repeating the first line almost note for note in the third, does not help to make it endurable. Sing it to an eight-line tune such as *Hyfrydol*.[1] At once its character is changed. It becomes a sustained, balanced unity. The reason may be made clear by a diagram. The hymn of eight verses is like Fig. 1. It has no pattern

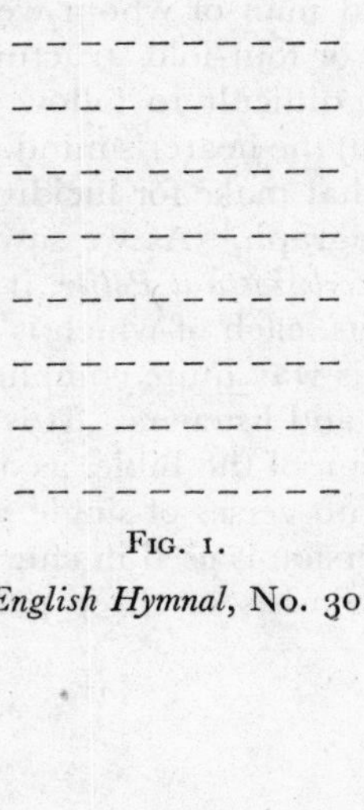

FIG. 1.

[1] *English Hymnal*, No. 301.

Join together each pair of verses. It looks like this :—

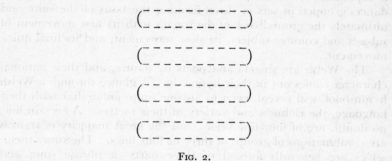

FIG. 2.

It now has a pattern, a construction which makes it able to be seen as a whole.

In the laws of thought in words, behind which are these laws of sight and sound, the same principle holds good. In grammar we learn that a sentence consists of a subject and a predicate, and if the predicate is transitive it must be followed by a third, the object. In its simplest form it is made up of a noun in the nominative, a verb, and another noun in the accusative case—*e.g.*, " The man gave a bone ". Adjectives may be added to the nouns and adverbs to the verb—*e.g.*, " The kind man often gave a nice bone ". A remote object with its adjective may be attached to the object, bringing the elements up to four—*e.g.*, " The kind man often gave a nice bone to the old dog "—but, with the additions, the sentence still preserves its three- or four-fold structure. Whole dependent clauses may be added—*e.g.*, " The kind man of whom we have just been talking, etc."—but if the three- or four-fold structure is broken the sentence becomes confused and difficult to follow. If it is preserved, the sentence remains clear in the hearer's mind. It is not so much short as balanced sentences that make for lucidity.

So, too, in the paragraph. As we saw in the example quoted above from Hooker's *Ecclesiastical Polity*, it should have a structure of three or four elements, each of which is compounded of three or more sentences. In this way quite complicated ideas can be taken in by ordinary readers and listeners. It is one of the grave defects of the Authorised Version of the Bible, as of cheap popular journalism, that it is cut up into verses of single sentences. On the other hand, if the Revised Version is used in church it will be noticed that the Lesson generally consists of three paragraphs, just as in the

Breviary Matins the lections are three in each nocturn. Again, in answering questions from the platform, or in letters to the Press, whence the reply is carried on beyond three sentences or groups of sentences it becomes too long, and only puzzles the questioner.

In works on a larger scale the same principle should prevail. A *Times* leading article is generally composed of three paragraphs, and we feel it has a unity and completeness that make it easy to read. A longer article in a magazine is made more readable if its several parts are divided and emphasised by the numerals I, II, III. We are helped in seeing the drift and plan of a book if in the table of contents the chapters to follow are analysed in three- or four-fold form. The three-volume novel took its shape because, like the three-act play, the first introduced us to the various characters, the second showed us complications arising from the interplay of their actions—new characters are, as a rule, not introduced—except for deliberate and special reasons—after the book or play has got under way—and the third gives us the solution of the problems raised.

So, many years ago, Aristotle, when lecturing on the Art of Poetry and the Nature of the Attic Drama, told his hearers that—

" the action represented must be complete, that is, it must have a beginning, a middle, and an end. It must not be a sort of composition in which one can see no reason why it should begin or end where it does. It must have a beginning which must be comparatively intelligible in itself, and does not forcibly provoke the question, ' How came all this to be ? ' ; an end which is satisfying and does not provoke the question ' And then ? ' ; and a middle which is necessitated by the beginning and necessitates the end." [1]

Illustrations of this " rule of three " might be multiplied almost indefinitely. Say a thing three times if you wish it to be remembered. The Bellman in *The Hunting of the Snark* was not epistemologically accurate when he announced that " what I tell you three times is true ".[2] It was a pragmatic idea of Truth that he held—namely, that what you can get people to believe is practically true, in this case the theory was that " the Führer is always

---

[1] A free rendering of, and comment on *Poetics*, VI, vii, 1 by W. D. Ross in his *Aristotle* (Methuen 1923), p. 281. As Buffon said : " There are so many works made up of shreds and patches, and so few moulded in a single casting. Every subject has a unity in itself and can be treated as a single theme. Without this the details become interruptions and the whole becomes confused and tedious instead of being a coherent and solid work." See p. 91 below.

[2] Lewis Carroll, *The Hunting of the Snark*.

right ", but it relied on a sound psychology. This, of course, can be overdone so as to produce exactly the opposite effect. Horace Walpole is quoted as saying of Dr. Johnson, whom he did not admire :—

> " His Essays I detest. They are full of what I call ' tripto-logy ', or repeating the same thing thrice over, so that three papers to the same effect might be made out of any one paper in *The Rambler*." [1]

But it works in most cases. [2]

In practical matters this " rule of three " is a useful guide. Always try a thing over three times before giving up, and you will feel that you have done your best : " try, try, try, again ", as William Edward Hickson once exhorted us. A choir should get a thing right after going through it thrice ; if it does not it is better to put it aside for a time ; next week its members will probably have learned it by automatic subconscious action. We might add that the

[1] Cp. T. Seccombe, *The Age of Johnson* (Bell, 1891–1938), p. 9. I cannot trace the passage, but in *The Letters of Horace Walpole, Fourth Earl of Oxford*, ed. Mrs. Paget Toynbee (Oxford, 1904), Vol. X, 1777–1779, No. 1922, Letter to the Countess of Upper Ossory, Feb. 1, 1779, p. 371, we read : "Another modern idol, far less deservedly enshrined (than Garrick), Dr. Johnson, I have been saying this morning, that the latter deals so much in triple tautology, or the fault of repeating the same sense in three different phrases, that I believe it would be possible, taking the groundwork for all three, to make one of his *Ramblers* into three different papers, that all should have exactly the same purport and meaning, but in different phrases. It would be a good trick for somebody to produce one and read it ; a second would say ' Bless me, I have this very paper in my pocket, but in quite another diction ' ; and so a third."

[2] " In writing, a thing three times said, and each time said badly, may be of more effect than that terse, full and final expression which the doctors rightly commend."—Sir Walter Raleigh, *Style* (Arnold, 1918), p. 109.

The power of visualising may slightly vary in individuals, and considerably in peoples. Germans seem to think more in sound. " *Hören sie mal*," they will say, where we ejaculate, " Look here " ; " *Ist Frau X zu sprechen?* " where we say, " Is Mrs. X. at home ? " or " Can I see Mrs. X ? " This possibly makes their writing more full and exact, but hinders their power of seeing things as a whole. They seem to be like people who take photographs with a too wide-angle lens, and get a mass of detail, but no picture. The French, on the other hand, seem to have a sharper, if more contracted, vision and a strong sense of proportion in language. " What is not clear is not French," said Antoine Rivarol (see below, Ch. IV, p. 65). Descartes held that things were true of which we had clear ideas. They rely on intuition and strict logic rather than on long-drawn-out arguments and emotional appeals, and turn from side issues. In the same way some people can hear higher notes than others and can distinguish the bat's cry, to which others are deaf. Such variations, however, are only very slight ; practically we can all see only one octave of colour and hear about seven octaves of sound.

experience of the law courts has led the orator at the Bar to introduce his case, plead its merits, and wind up with a peroration; but we will take our further illustration from the art of teaching.

It has been the ruin of Germany that for over a hundred years she has followed the educational theories of Fichte in his *Address to the German Nation*—viz., that education means the training of one class of students to command and the other to obey [1]—instead of following those of Herbart and Pestalozzi, based on a sounder psychology. The Herbartian method of preparing and giving lessons rested on a sound understanding of human nature. It roughly consisted of three stages, at any rate as formulated by his disciples.

(*a*) The first was the presentation of the subject so as to concentrate attention on the particular matter in hand and to call up an " apperception mass " of already acquired information to set the new knowledge in relation to it.

(*b*) The second consisted in imparting of this new knowledge and in guiding of the pupil's mind to further facts and ideas.

(*c*) Finally there came the application of them to the conduct of life and the assimilating of them by the pupil's mind. This, he urged, was best done by action, by verification, by experiments, by the pupil taking phrases on to his own lips, and by all that has come to be known as " expression work ".[2]

This is all effective because it is based on a sound psychology of interest and emotion. The appeal is made first to the imagination, the calling up of things already known and giving them " feeling tone " ; then by an appeal to the natural activities of the intellect, finding out new facts, judging and criticising them, asking and answering questions; then by the exercise of the will, assimilating what has been acquired and making it your own.

The close parallel of the Ignatian method of meditation will be obvious to many, but a theological student who practises meditation

[1] Werke (Leipzig, 1849), *Reden an die deutsche Nation*, " Zweite Rede," p. 281 : " The new education must consist in this, that it undertakes this reconstruction on the ground of entirely destroying the freedom of the will, so as to give firm certainty of decision and make impossible any opposition of will so that it can be reckoned, and relied, on." Quoted on p. 10 of my *Nietzsche or Christ* (S.P.C.K., " Little Books on Religion," No. 166, 1940).

[2] Herbart wrote at great length, and is not always concise or clear. His teaching can be found summarised in J. J. Findlay's *Principles of Class Teaching* (Macmillan, 1902), Section IV, " Method," Ch. XIII, " The Acquisition of Knowledge—Steps followed in the Process," pp. 313-333. Herbart's actual stages were five in number, but that was because he divided into two the first and the last of the three stages of the above outline.

needs a warning. While ultimately it will help his preaching, all thought of so using it should be put aside while at his devotions. Even if thoughts " dart " he should not make notes of them. This is the one exception to the rule of bringing out your note-book to enter them. They will most probably come again, but in any case he cannot afford to use his meditation as a sort of preparation for homiletics.

So in making a sermon *first see it in outline and in an outline of three or* (if the middle is divided into two sections) *of four parts.*

The aim of the Introduction or first part is to present a background against which the rest may be displayed, to bring into the forefront of the minds of the congregation that which they already know, and to which you wish to add the new ideas already in your own mind. This should normally be a New, or Old, Testament story, retold to lead up to and stress the main idea that you wish to be in their minds for the next quarter of an hour. So, long ago, Plato said :—

> " I would observe that discourse and vocal utterance of any kind have their preludes, their preliminaries as I might say, preliminaries—which furnish a useful methodical introduction to the coming performance." [1]

The story may be quite familiar to yourself, but it is never safe to attribute knowledge of any sort to the members of your congregation. Intelligence they will have, and we generally under-rate how much, but familiarity with particular parts of the Bible it is never safe to assume. I once in class proposed making a sermon on the story of Naaman, and asked for suggestions as to the treatment of the subject and lessons that might be drawn from it. I was met with a stony silence, till one of the students plucked up courage and asked, " Please, sir, what *is* the story of Naaman? " When next year I repeated the lecture I took the precaution of first reading the story out. Normally, I say, the Introduction should consist of the re-telling of some story in the Bible, but equally well it may give the background of the occasion on which some saying was uttered; or possibly it may be better to introduce the subject by some event in history or some recent occurrence in political or social life.[2]

---

[1] *Laws*, Bk. IV, p. 722, tr. A. E. Taylor (Dent, 1934), p. 107.

[2] As examples of introductions to analyse and with which to practise delivery in church, I have found the following useful, for re-telling a story from the Gospels to introduce a special point :—

Phillips Brooks, *Make the Men Sit Down, Twenty Sermons* (Macmillan, 1899), Sermon XIII, p. 226.

Then deal with the second part. This is the place for the appeal to the intellect, for teaching. Explain the meaning of the passage to your hearers to add to their knowledge. If, for instance, you are preaching on the parable of the "Unjust" Steward, or rather the steward " of unrighteousness ", explain from your commentary the conditions of estate management in Palestine in our Lord's time, and clear up the difficulty people find when they think that Christ approved of cheating.[1] Illustrate your theme by parallels in daily life, or by examples from history, or stories from books.[2] Liddon's *Christ in the Storm* aimed at showing from three examples in the past that Christ was not forsaking his Church as if asleep when she was in peril. Meet objections that may be raised, and so anticipate the arguments of the Rationalist Press Association; give constructive arguments (*e.g.*) on the evidence for the Resurrection of our Lord or for belief in the life after death. Enforce your contentions by quotations showing how learned men have said, and said better, what you are trying to say, or quote from poets who have put it in better words than you can muster.[3] There should be an ample store of such illustrations and quotations from your note-book, which have accumulated where you have filed them. They should be drawn from all sources and from various departments of life, reading, and

---

Liddon, " Christ in the Storm," *University Sermon, Second Series* (Rivingtons, 1883), Sermon IX, p. 103.

For a sermon based on knowledge of human nature, J. H. Newman, *The Religious Use of Excited Feelings.*

For a sermon dealing with practical problems of life, F. W. Robertson, " Triumph over Hindrances—Zaccheus," *Sermons, First Series* (Kegan Paul, 1899), No. V, preached October 20, 1850, p. 70; " Christ's Judgment concerning Inheritance," *ibid., Second Series*, No. I, preached June 22, 1851.

[1] Cp. H. Latham, *Pastor Pastorum* (Cambridge, 1904), pp. 386–393, and quoting Edersheim, *Life and Times of Jesus the Messiah* (Longmans, 1891), Vol. II, p. 267.

[2] Cp. Geo. Herbert, *The Priest to the Temple, or the Countrey Parson*, Ch. VII, " The Parson Preaching ": " Particulars ever touch, and awake more than generals. . . . Sometimes he tells them stories, and sayings of others, according as his text invites him; for them also men heed, and remember better than exhortations; which though earnest yet often die with the sermon, especially with countrey people, which are thick, and heavy, and hard to raise to a point of Zeal, and Fervency, and need a mountain of fire to kindle them; but stories and sayings they will well remember."

[3] Cp. Cicero, *Orator*, XXXIV, 120: " Commemoratio autem antiquitatis exemplorumque prolatio summa cum delectatione et auctoritatem orationi affert et fidem." (Moreover, the mention of antiquity and the citation of examples gives the speech authority and credibility as well as affording the highest pleasure to the audience.)

experience. The aim of this part of the sermon is to teach and to make people think. The language should be that of ordinary daily intercourse in life.[1] In it the preacher should, so to speak, get down from the pulpit, and out of the church into the world, in order that he may bring back the men and things he finds there into the house of God and before the altar.

This last should be the aim of the third part. If possible it should have as its purpose that of getting people to do something definite. Mark Antony when he made his speech to his " friends, Romans, countrymen " knew exactly what he wanted them to do, and though he disclaimed the intention of rousing them to a sudden flood of mutiny, knew also from the beginning how to weld his words together and bring them to a climax at the end. Where there is policy and plan in parish work, sermons can further its end, and will become much more interesting when they lead up to some " expression work " to follow, and people are expected to do something as a consequence of listening. But in most cases the end is to teach and drive home some idea. Here again their effect can be enhanced by a suitable choice of hymn and collect to follow. But this, of course, necessitates the choosing of a subject as well as the hymns considerably more than a week ahead.

So a sermon in the pulpit, like a lawyer's plea in the courts, ends naturally in some sort of a peroration with an appeal to the feelings. This partly because, as notably in an hour's lecture, attention begins to flag at the end of the time allotted.

The " curve of attention " has been worked out by experts in psychology and in the art of teaching. At first it is apt to fall, and needs to be supported by emphasis and interest. Hence the need of the Introduction. As time goes on, if the matter is well arranged and one thing leads on to another, less effort is needed to attend, and the tone of the speaker must still be clear, but may be with less emphasis. Then towards the end the mind grows tired, and in the application a stronger emotional note may be struck to stimulate it, while a few minutes before the end attention revives again, and can be raised to a still higher pitch of receptiveness by an impassioned

---

[1] Cp. Pascal, *Pensées*, No. 18, ed. Brunschvicg : " La manière d'écrire d'Épictète, de Montaigne, et de Salomon de Tultie [(*i.e.*, of Pascal himself] est la plus d'usage, qui insinue le mieux, qui demeure plus dans la mémoire, et qui se fait le plus citer, parce qu'elle est toute composée de pensées nées sur le sentretiens ordinaires de la vie." (The manner in which Epictetus, Montaigne, and Salomon de Tultie wrote, is the most usual, the most suggestive, the most remembered, and oftenest quoted ; because it is entirely composed of thoughts born from the common talk of life.)

peroration driving home the main purpose of what has been said.[1] " L'Éloquence continue ennuie," wrote Pascal (Sustained eloquence bores us),[2] and he knew how to appeal to men. The constant exhortation we generally hear from the pulpit defeats its own end. A case first built up by a quiet appeal to imagination and reason can then be driven home by an appeal to the emotions and the will.

All this depends on the sermon being framed in a pattern with balance and proportion, and this implies a unity in the outline. There should be one idea running through all, while each part should be complete in itself. Therefore a title should be thought of which sums up the main idea as if the sermon were going to be published in print. This will probably be the heading under which the various entries were made in the loose-leaf note-book. But the end should be in the mind of the preacher as the final cause from the beginning.[3]

[1] Cp. J. Adams, *Exposition and Illustration in Teaching* (Macmillan, 1909–1923), p. 381.

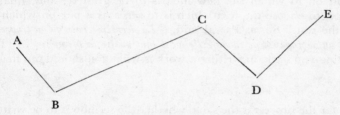

" The work begins at A and for a little time, through distraction and the effort to concentrate, there is a slight diminution of efficiency in work. At B the practice effect beings to tell, and the line gradually rises to C. At this point the practice effect is counterbalanced by the fatigue effect, that goes on increasing while the practice effect cannot increase further. The result is that there is a gradual falling off of the effectiveness of the work till we reach D. Here the prospect of a speedy release from effort, along with a quickening of the conscience in view of the approaching end of further opportunity, gives a little fillip to the student, and his effectiveness rises somewhat to the end, E."

[2] *Pensées*, No. 355.

[3] Cp. Swift, " Pulpit Eloquence," *The Tatler*, No. 66. " He [Dr. Atterbury] has a peculiar force in his way, and has charmed many of his audience, who could not be intelligent hearers of his discourse were there not explanation as well as grace in his action. This art of his is useful with the most exact and honest skill: he never attempts your passions until he has convinced your reason. All the objections which he can form are laid open and dispersed before he uses the least vehemence in his sermon; but when he thinks he has your head, he very soon wins your heart; and never pretends to show the beauty of holiness until he has convinced you of the truth of it."

D

The sermon should work up to a definite point. To secure this it is as well to write at the head of the outline not only the title but the aim of the sermon, just as in a case-paper used in social work the help asked for by the applicant should be supplemented by a note of the plan adopted at least in the mind of the worker, even if it cannot be clearly stated in a few words. This is not always possible. Often the aim of the sermon is merely to teach something and to leave a definite idea in the mind of the congregation, but to try to define the aim will help to give point and definition to the whole. The actual text is often the last thing to be chosen as the writer of an article in a magazine chooses the title or motto, out of the many that may have occurred to him, which seems to sum up best the gist of the whole.

Thus the mental process is *to begin at the end*, and to think first of what you want to get understood or done, then to think of reasons or arguments to support it or of objections to be removed; after that to call up what the hearer already knows, to use it as the body of thought on to which the new idea is to be grafted; and, finally, perhaps, to choose the text which is to serve as a peg on which to hang the rest. So, as Pascal said, " *La dernière chose qu'on trouve en faisant un ouvrage est de savoir celle qu'il faut mettre la première* ". (The last thing you settle in writing a work is what you should put first.)[1]

IV

So far the process is the same whether the sermon is to be written out or to be preached *ex tempore* from the outline. Later on it will become more natural—sometimes, at least—to preach without manuscript, perhaps even without notes, before you; but it will always be best to think of your matter as seen in outline. Even when it has become more natural for a preacher to find his words at the moment of delivery, he will be well advised always to have some writing work on hand, if only as a check on diffuseness or bad habits in grammar, *aposiopeseis* or false concords. All the thinking out of the sermon should have been done at home and with a pen in his hand, for, as Bacon warned us, if " Reading maketh a full man; Conference a ready man "; it is writing that makes " an exact man ".[2]

The preacher, in making his outline, has, of course, heard as well as seen his matter, and has, so to speak, taken notes from himself; but now he should imagine his congregation before him and set

---

[1] *Pensées*, No. 19.   [2] *Essay* 50, " Of Studies."

himself to hear himself speaking to them. Jane Taylor, who knew so well how to write her *Poems for Infant Minds* so that children would listen and delight in them, tells us how she set to work. She imagined she had what Lamb would have called a " dream child " before her, and would address her. When she grew tired and felt her inspiration flagging she would say, " There, love, now you may go." [1] Mrs. Turner, the creator of the " Cautionary Story ", a new art-form, at the beginning of the nineteenth century, told in a tale " How to Write a Letter " that :—

> " Maria intended a letter to write,
> But could not begin, as she thought, to indite.
> So she went to her mother with pencil and slate
> Containing ' Dear Sister ', and also a date.
>
> " ' With nothing to say, my dear girl, do not think
> Of wasting your time over paper and ink;
> But certainly this is an excellent way
> To try with your slate to find something to say.'
>
> " ' I will give you a rule,' said her mother. ' My dear,
> Just think for a moment your sister is here.
> And what would you tell her?   Consider, and then,
> Though silent your tongue, you can speak with your pen.' " [2]

The sermon-writer should do likewise. He should, as we saw, resist the temptation to add new matter to what he already has in his outline. He will find it makes a new patch on the pattern and will distort the scheme. The new ideas that obtrude as he writes will side-track attention. On reading over what he has written he will generally find that he has, after all, to cut out these little additions. It will be no real loss. People can take in only a certain amount at a time, and if that is coherent, and if he has got over to them what he has in his outline, the chances are that they, too, will think for themselves the further thoughts that it suggested to him.

This will keep him speaking in the common language of ordinary

[1] Ann Taylor, in her *Autobiography*, gives the following account of her sister's method of composition, which goes to show that, young as she was, she had already divined the only way in such an enterprise: " I have heard Jane say, when sitting down to our new evening's business, ' I try to conjure up some child into my presence, address her suitably, as well as I am able, and when I begin to flag, I say to her, " There, love, now you may go." —*The " Original Poems " and Others by Ann and Jane Taylor and Adelaide O'Keeffe*, ed. E. V. Lucas (Wells, Gardner, Darton and Co.), Introduction, p. xvi.
[2] Cp. *Jane Austen : Her Life and Letters*.   W. Austen Leigh and R. A. Austen Leigh (Smith Elder, 1913), p. 157: " I have now attained the true art of letter writing, which we are always told is to express on paper exactly what we would say to the same person by word of mouth."

men. There are certain obvious differences between the speech of mutual conversation and that of continuous exposition, just as there are between things said and those read from print. Somehow the use of the first personal pronoun, while it sounds modest and deprecatory on the platform, and if it is uttered in the right tone in conversation is unassuming, in the pulpit sounds arrogant " as who should say I am Sir Oracle ". There, as Pascal wrote, " *Le moi est haïssable* ".[1] This does not mean that the preacher should be slangy or talk down to what he supposes to be his hearers' ordinary level of speech. The recent advice of a certain bishop that the parson in the pulpit should speak like the man in the street was clearly wrong. It would not be conciliating to drop his " h "s, nor to employ the adjective that so many think it necessary to attach to nearly everything they speak of, but he will avoid using unfamiliar words not in the vocabulary of his hearers and technical terms he has not time to explain. He will not use many abstract terms which mean much to himself but little to his hearers before they are familiar with the many concrete instances from which they have been drawn out. He will write in shorter paragraphs and speak in shorter sentences. What is jerky and bald when read is often steady and adequate when spoken. But you may use quite a number of unfamiliar terms and be understood if your outline is clear and the general drift of what you say is plain.

This will entail scope for variety in pace and in tone. What you say will not be monotonous if you hear yourself as you write. There is a difference between telling a story, arguing a point, urging to conviction, and quoting an authority. This will come of itself, and will not be an oratorical diction stuck on. At the same time it will

---

[1] Cp. *Pensées*, No. 455. The *Logique de Port Royal* (III. 19): " Feu M. Pascal, qui savait autant de véritable rhétorique que personne en ait jamais su, portait cette regle (Ne point parler de soi) jusque à prétendre qu'un honnête homme devait éviter de se nommer, et même de se servir des mots de *je* et de *moi*, et il avait accoutumé de dire a ce sujet que la piété chrétienne anéantit le *moi* humain et que la civilité humaine le cache et le supprime." (The late M. Pascal, who knew more about true rhetoric than any one else ever knew, carried this rule (of not speaking of yourself) so far as to claim that a gentleman ought to avoid speaking about himself, and not even use the words I and Me, and he used to say on this matter that Christian piety brought to nothing the human " Me " and that human civilisation hid it and suppressed it.)

The English method of substituting " I knew a man who " for " I " is a well-known paraphrase for the first personal pronoun in the pulpit.

M. Le Chevallier de Méré said that the Honnête Homme (or gentleman) did not say " *je* " but " *on* ". " One " in English is awkward. " We ", or the more idiomatic " you ", is rather the English use.

be personal, because it will be what you heard yourself say as you wrote, and the variety was in the matter with which you dealt.

To deliver a sermon with conscious art is not theatrical or insincere, for a preacher who does so is re-enacting his own ideas and feelings. He is going back to states of thought and emotion deliberately intended to be reproduced, later on, in the people he addresses. It is wrong only if it is made a substitute for genuine conviction in order to save the labour of thought and the trouble of preparation.[1]

But the general principles are, I feel sure, sound. When a man has made an outline, and has put down the essentials of what he wants to say, his work becomes easy. As Buffon saw,

> " he enjoys writing. Ideas come spontaneously to birth. Words flow freely. His style becomes natural and easy. He warms to his subject. His matter takes on colour. Feeling and insight grow and carry him on. What he has said leads him on to what he goes on to say, and his style becomes interesting, luminous, and brilliant." [2]

All this is some of the technique of sermon preparation. It is a method by which the young preacher would do well to discipline himself. There is, I think, no fear of a too rigid following of what has been said. Every man is different and has different ways, but it is well to have certain lines to begin on which can afterwards be modified and developed as each finds best for himself. For, to quote Buffon again :—

> " Well-written works are the only works that live for posterity. Knowledge, wealth, numbers, masses, originality, or novelty of facts give no guarantee of immortality. Works that deal with small matters, without taste, nobility, or genius, pass away or are better treated by others more clever. All these things are from outside the man. *Style is (of) the man himself.*" [3]

[1] Cp. Whately, *Elements of Rhetoric*, Pt. IV, Ch. iii. § 10, says that such a preacher " will appear to be speaking, because he actually *will be* speaking the sentiments, not indeed which at that time first *arise* in his own mind, but which are then really *present* to, and occupy, his mind ".

[2] Below p. 91.

[3] Below p. 93. " Les ouvrages bien écrits seront les seuls qui passeront à la posterité.—Ces choses sont hors de l'homme. Le Style est (de) l'homme même."

III

THE STORAGE OF MATERIAL

" Primum enim aliter utimur propriis, aliter commodatis, longeque interesse manifestum est possideat quis quae profert and mutuetur." (The use we make of what belongs to ourselves is quite different from our use of what we take on loan : there is obviously a wide gulf between owning what we give out and borrowing it from others.)—Tacitus, *Dialogus de Oratoribus*, tr. Sir William Peterson, (Loeb edition), Ch. 32, p. 98.

" I am aware indeed that the transferring of the things we read and learn into commonplace books is thought by some to be detrimental to learning, as retarding the course of the reader and inviting the memory to take holiday. Nevertheless, as it is but a counterfeit thing in knowledge to be forward and pregnant, except a man be also deep and full, I hold diligence and labour in the entry of commonplaces to be a matter of great use and support in studying; as that which supplies matter to invention, and contracts the sight of the judgment to a point."—Bacon, *De Augmentis Scientiarum*, Ch. V.

" Was du ererbt von deinen Vätern hast,
Erwirb es um es zu besitzen."
(There is none
Is rightful Lord of his Inheritance
Till what he had is by new toil re-won.)
—Goethe, *Faust*, tr. G. M. Cookson (Routledge's Broadway Translations, 1927), p. 33.

So far we have been thinking of the preacher and the workings of his mind. We have considered them in the making of the single sermon, and on the analogy of the schoolmaster preparing his lesson.

But he will soon, as does the teacher in school, find his material growing beyond what he can use on any one single occasion, and will realise his opportunities for work on a larger scale. He will find that he must sort his notes so that he can put his finger on what he wants when opportunity comes for him to use it. He will soon realise the need of co-ordinating separate ideas and getting them into order. He will find it necessary to plan his whole field of thought so as to become a mentally integrated man. He will find it necessary for himself, as the schoolmaster sees his need of a syllabus, and, working by it, finds the school-term all too short. He will aim at continuity and fullness in his preaching, and there will be for him no " perplexity " what to preach about, except that which comes from having more to say than is possible in what he will soon come to feel as the limited opportunities of the pulpit.

But he must also think of his hearers and ask himself what has been the result of all sermons they have heard. " Our religion is in a book," said Dr. Johnson. "We have an order of men whose duty it is to teach it; we have one day in the week set apart for it, and this is in general pretty well observed; yet ask the first ten gross men you meet, and hear what they can tell of their religion." The theological ignorance of the masses, most of whom have heard many sermons, amazes us. Distinguished exponents of Natural Science and well-known authors of Fiction contribute to books declaring, " What I Believe ", and reveals an almost absolute ignorance of what Christianity really is. Brains Trusts composed of well-known writers, artists, and politicians have nothing to say when an inquirer asks, " What first set things moving? " as if Aristotle and Aquinas, to say nothing of the compiler of the Book of Genesis, had never existed. Thousands of children who have been to Sunday School seem to have learned nothing and, what is more serious, millions have been taught by trained teachers and have got a very fair knowledge of the Bible, but seem to be quite in the dark as to the meaning of the Creed or as to what goes on in church, while the excellent training in character that so many have received is for the most part unreasoned and vague. Anyone who has set himself to " meet objections " at a " Padre's Hour " in the Army, or who has taken part in the discussions that go on, day in day out, in Hyde Park and other gathering places in our large cities, will realise how we have in most cases entirely failed to " get it over ".

Therefore—it is the old tale—we must look ahead more. Planning the future by a longer span in our work is necessary. I have often urged this with regard to parish work generally.[1] There is the same need for it for the preacher. For his own sake, to save unnecessary worry and labour, to direct his efforts to a point, to do his work thoroughly, he must work on a larger scale. Still more for the sake of his congregation must he build up on a foundation already laid, and must enlarge their " apperception mass " so that they understand better whatever he may tell them that is new. He must increase their whole field of religious thought. By continued, coherent work he will strengthen their interest and quicken their understanding. He will familiarise them slowly with terms which at present often convey no meaning to them at all.

[1] Cp. my *Pastoral Theology and the Modern World* (Oxford, 1920), Ch. I, " The Span of Work."

Among the theological students in their first year at King's College we found that they missed much of the benefit they might have gained from lectures because of their unfamiliarity with technical theological terms. They did not know, at any rate till they had stopped to think about it, what was the difference between Theism and Deism, what was meant by Immanence and by Transcendence, what were the relations between Reason and Relevation. So we started in the preliminary year a course of simple apologetic lectures mainly to familiarise them with certain terms, so that afterwards we could use them without fear of their failing to convey any definite meaning. We cannot order our congregations to come to a course of preliminary instruction, but we can see to it that we do not use too many abstract words ending in " ion ", or too many technical terms ending in " -ology ", until (by explanation, by concrete examples, or by making our hearers familiar, in earlier sermons, with the language of Theology) we are pretty sure that they know what we mean.[1]

I

We want to get continuity and coherence in our preaching. This concerns both preacher and congregation. The young sermon-writer soon realises how little can be got into one homily. A service should generally last just less than sixty minutes, for the hour seems to be the normal unit of attention and effort. Preaching at the Eucharist is but one element in a larger whole, and the sermon should generally not take up more time than a quarter of an hour. After Evensong it may last longer—some twenty-five to thirty minutes, without making the whole exceed an hour. If it is constructed as we have suggested above, some three or four of these minutes are taken up by the introduction, by getting the attention of the congregation, by recalling familiar ideas to their minds, and some three or four by the application, summing up what has been said, directing it to a point and inciting to action; this leaves but

[1] " Do not spend your sermons in general and indefinite things, as in exhortations to people to get Christ, to be united to Christ, and things of like unlimited signification; but tell them in every duty what are the measures, what circumstances, what instruments, and what is the particular minute meaning of every general advice. For generals not explicated do but fill people's heads with empty notions, and their mouths with perpetual unintelligible talk; but their hearts remain empty, and themselves are not edified."—Jeremy Taylor, *Rules and advices to the Clergy of the Diocese of Down and Connor for their deportment in their personal and public Capacities*, IV, " Rules and advice, concerning preaching," xlii, *Works* (London, 1854), Vol. I, p. 107.

ten to fifteen minutes for introducing new ideas and for continuous teaching to be carried on from sermon to sermon.

Of course those ten or fifteen minutes will suggest more than there has been time to say. If the words have started men thinking, they will add for themselves much that the preacher would have liked to say for himself. So if his main lines are clear he need not be afraid of leaving things out. Relevant additions will probably occur to his hearers of themselves later on, and more securely than if he had overloaded his matter with detail. To exhaust a subject, it has been said, is to exhaust your audience. The middle of the sermon should not attempt to deal with more than three (or four) main new facts or illustrations. That, as we saw, is as much as the ordinary man can take in at one time.[1]

Therefore there is all the more reason to arrange your material well ahead. This is what makes the difference always between casual and high-class work. The mere casual labourer lives from day to day in work and in wage; the artisan plans his work, and gets his pay, by the week. The middleman and manager, engaged in distribution, anticipate the changes of season, and earn a salary paid by the month; the administrator thinks in terms of the year; while the scholar and the writer find a lifetime too short for their work. The preacher should be at least of the class of the teacher, with his yearly syllabus and stipend, if not of the scholar who, like Ignatius, is still a disciple at the end of his days.[2]

Therefore, as the material of what he wants to say, because he has made it his own, accumulates, he should *sort it and file it in a mental and physical framework.*

The first step is taken with the single sermon. He feels it is inadequate. He has accumulated too much to get into it. He must select what matters most; the rest he can leave for another time—for another year, perhaps. He is preaching, say, on Low Sunday. On Easter Day the significance of the Resurrection has been spoken about. Is the evidence for the fact sufficient? He has

---

[1] " The Parson exceeds not an hour in preaching, because all ages have thought that a competency, and he that profits not in that time will less afterward; the same affection which made him not profit before, making him then weary, and so he grows from not relishing to loathing."—George Herbert, *The Countrey Parson*, Ch. VII, " The Parson Preaching."

Cp. my " The Psychology of Preaching, Evangelism, and Education," in *Psychology and the Church*, ed. O. Hardmann (Macmillan, 1925), pp. 165–167.

[2] *Ad Romanos*, V, 7. " Now I am beginning to be a disciple "; cp. Eusebius, *Ecclesiastical History*, Bk. III, 36, 9.

studied it at College only a few years before, and here is his subject for Low Sunday. (Remember he is thinking about it early in Lent, a month before.) He will reproduce what he learned as a student. He finds that a bare outline is as much as he can get in. But no subject is fully dealt with till we have heard the other side and have met objections and criticisms, such as that " it all happened so long ago ". That must be left for another time—for one of the Sundays after Easter if he has got his material ready; for next year, if, as is probably the case, he needs more time to get it up.

Then, maybe, when he has put his subject aside for a time and his brain is incubating, he is reading H. M. Gwatkins' *The Knowledge of God*, and he comes across the words:—

" Root out once for all from your mind any lurking idea that historical evidence is made uncertain by lapse of time."

He reads on—how it can be lost or destroyed—how historical criticism can deal with difficulties almost as effectively after twenty years as after two; he notes his illustrations; he selects three or four with which he is already familiar; and he has more than enough matter for his sermon to prove that it is an utter fallacy to imagine, as many do, that history steadily becomes more uncertain as we trace it backwards into what are metaphorically called " the mists of antiquity ", and is able to reassure his congregation that the Gospel records are not unreliable,[1] and that, as Sir Frederic Kenyon, the

---

[1] H. M. Gwatkin, *The Knowledge of God* (T. & T. Clark, 1906), Vol. I, p. 192. The whole passage runs: " Root out once for all from your mind any lurking idea that historical evidence is made uncertain by lapse of time. There is a change when the doctrine is no longer backed up by living memory; but after that there is little further change. If writings are lost or mutilated, whatever remains, remains exactly what it was at first. If texts become corrupt in course of time, words fall out of use, and manners of ways and thinking change, these are difficulties with which historical criticism can deal almost as effectively after twenty years as after two. The number of the Beast was exactly the puzzle to Irenaeus that it is to us; and Augustine's nearness to the Gospel gave him scarcely any advantage above our own for understanding it. Nor do the changes bear much relation to the lapse of time. The old Greeks are easier to understand than the men of the Middle Ages; and the Laws of Hammurabi seem scarcely more obscure than the Dooms of Alfred. We have more in common with Pericles and Caesar than with Karl the Great or Nicephorus Phocas. The Old Testament bears the mark of the unchanging East, and the Apostolic Age is in many ways more modern than the eighteenth century. It is utter fallacy to imagine, as many do, that history steadily becomes more uncertain as we trace it backwards into what are metaphorically called the mists of antiquity."

Cp. my *The Case for Miracle* (S.P.C.K., 1936), Ch. III, " Non-Christian Theories of the Resurrection," pp. 72–76.

former Keeper of the MSS. in the British Museum, writes in his *Our Bible and the Ancient Manuscripts* (last words) :—

" The general reader may be confident that he has nothing to fear from the fullest and freest research; that he may, on the contrary, expect a constant accession of knowledge and of interest, and that in the end truth will prevail." [1]

But before quoting this he must have read up the subject for himself and have " verified his references "—a thing he cannot do in a week.

He should therefore arrange his sermons in groups of three or four. This will make it easier for himself, and save him the worry of thinking, " What shall I preach about? " He had better not announce them as " a course ", for, somehow, the word has a forbidding sound, but the connection should be in his own mind, and will be in the minds of his hearers, making what he says easier to understand, and therefore more interesting, because it comes to a continually growing " apperception mass ". If the " course " is a failure he can carry it through if it is one of only three or four, while if it gets home he can always add on others to supplement it or complete what he has tried to say. But in casting the series he should try to estimate whether it seems likely to do what he is aiming at.

The parish priest will soon feel the necessity of concentration on the essentials of the Faith. So little can be done in the pulpit that he must keep to what matters most in the Christian Creed. Many interesting and useful subjects must perforce be left out—the nature of Hebrew poetry, the character and aim of Jewish prophecy, the stories of the Old Testament and their true value and right interpretation, the priority of Ezra or Nehemiah, the composition of the Pentateuch, even important questions of apologetics, since the refutation of error is, after all, not so important as the establishment of truth. So, very soon, the need of classes will be felt where details can be entered into, and which can be followed by questions and discussion. There we can find out the matter of which we think men know, but of which as a matter of fact they don't. " It was a very interesting sermon, all about the Atonement," said a young student of my acquaintance to her aunt, " but," she added, " he never told us what the Atonement was." In classes we can discuss the things that really matter. We shall find out, for instance, how the question of free will, which we never thought of preaching about

[1] Fourth Edition, 1839, Vol. I, p. 254.

in the pulpit, has always been the enemy and underlies almost half
the " difficulties " about Christianity.[1] But mere military " Padre's
Hours " and civil " Brains Trusts " are, we shall find, not enough.
Something of the nature of Study Circles or Adult Education Classes
will be wanted, in which there is a background of literature and of
books read as well as discussed, and not mere " Classes for Sunday-
School Teachers ". But in all these, it would seem, the starting-
point is the sermon, to which people already come.

We shall realise, then, the ignorance of the general public, the
need for a grounding in religious teaching in the schools, of knowledge of the Bible, of the Prayer Book and of Church Services, of
Moral Theology, and of the Ten Commandments. We assume when
we refer to Nebuchadnezzar that people will know whom we are
talking about, but it is very doubtful whether they do, and we can
hardly spare time for a sermon to draw the lesson of the image that
he set up and the refusal of Shadrach, Meshach and Abednego to
bow down to the symbol of the Totalitarian State. All that should
have been done in school, and the preacher will realise that we must
have Church Schools, and will want to take part in the teaching
given in them.

We shall realise, too, the proper relation of the sermon to parish
work. If something to be done in the parish is explained in the
pulpit it will greatly increase the interest of what is said there. If
things are arranged ahead the hymns can be chosen to enforce the
preaching, can be published in the Parish Magazine, and learned in
time—perhaps in congregational practices, in which their meaning
can be explained. We could print there a short syllabus or outline
of what we are going to say, as University Extension Lecturers issue
a syllabus of their course beforehand. We could insert, after sermons have been preached, the quotations we made, so that our
hearers can have the exact words for themselves. We can back up
our words by literature, by having, and calling attention to, pamph-
lets on sale in the tract-rack at the doors, which can be passed on to
others, or by reference to books which can be borrowed from the
Public Library. We can stimulate the circulation of Church papers
and magazines. We can send letters to the Press (always taking
care how we write them and getting someone to " vet " them first),
and so carry on a wide propaganda. But the *starting-point is the
scheme of sermons prepared beforehand, and on a plan.*

[1] Cp. my *Free Will and Determinism* (S.P.C.K. " Little Books on Religion ",
No. 163, 1939), and *Lectures in Hyde Park* (S.P.C.K., 1927), Series II,
Lecture V, pp. 9–39.

II

Continuity and coherence in his work will prove of great value in its reaction on the character of the preacher himself. Study is always of greater interest, and therefore easier, if you are going to do something with what you learn. The final cause always works more strongly than the originating or first cause. A man will make a better student if he is going to preach, and preach continuously, and on a plan; and still better, *a fortiori*, if he is going to teach in class, to write for the Press or in books; and perhaps best of all if he is going to answer men's questions in public discussion. Even if his answers do not prove of much help to his questioners, their questions will be invaluable for his own education. Dialectic, after all, was the foundation of philosophy that Socrates laid.

The clergy are continually being exhorted to " keep up their reading ", and it may be a good thing for a boy to have the free run of a library and to browse at will among books. But this is probably the case only if at the same time he is under a discipline at school that will make him learn application and order. In later life such reading is apt to become desultory. A priest reads the paper to keep in touch with the world and to avoid getting an " ecclesiastical mind ", and novels to learn what are the aims and tastes of the ordinary man. Bishop King, it is said, used to advise his clergy to study moral theology in " the Bible, Aristotle's *Ethics*, and good novels "—excellent advice if the first two are seriously studied " with a commentary ".[1] Otherwise general reading is apt to become diffuse and superficial. There seems to be no reason for attacking any subject seriously.

Many of us who are older realise in looking back that in all these later years almost the only times that we have really thrashed out a subject for ourselves have been when we were going to preach or lecture upon it and realised in good time that we did not know it thoroughly enough to speak with authority, that we had not verified our references, or could not answer objections if they were made. For, to justify the preaching of a sermon, we should be able, if called upon, to quote our authorities, should know what recent thought has said on the subject, should be sure that we have got our facts right, that we have got that feeling, easily recognisable, when justified, that we really know our subject and can speak on it clearly and with ease.

[1] So Dr. Johnson to Boswell, *Life*, May 29, 1776. Vol. III, p. 58. " To be sure, Sir! I would have you read the Bible with a Commentary."

Right preparation for preaching will give direction and point to our reading. It will decide for us why we should read one kind of book rather than another. It will send us to big books if we make it a rule to make no statement from what we heard in lectures, or thought out for ourselves, without corroborating it by at least one independent authority. We need not quote this authority in the sermon—that might sound pedantic—but we should know where to find it and feel unsatisfied without having it somewhere where we could turn it up if challenged on the point in question. If, for instance, a man is preaching on Immortality, he would do well to read again Plato's *Phaedo*, A. Seth Pringle Pattison's Gifford Lectures *The Idea of Immortality* (Oxford, 1922), or, say, B. H. Streeter's symposium *Immortality* (Macmillan, 1917), or to read over again the first chapter of Butler's *Analogy*, " Of a Future Life ", or Tennyson's *In Memoriam* or Browning's *La Saisiaz*, or the article in Hastings' *Encyclopaedia of Religion and Ethics*, or that in the *Encyclopaedia Britannica*, or one of the authorities there referred to. These last would probably be accessible in his town Public Library.[1]

Such reading should be thorough. Notes should be made, even if not kept. Quotations should be copied out for possible use, and copied in their context. There should be always at least one such subject being prepared, even if it is supplemented by a considerable amount of lighter and casual reading.

This, at any rate, is the experience of many of us—that we do any thorough study only when we are preparing to preach, lecture, write, or answer question. " Enseigner ", writes Joubert, " c'est apprendre deux fois." [2] We are challenged, say, on the question of God's foreknowledge and man's free will. We dig out what Origen, Augustine, Boethius, Aquinas, Martineau and living writers have said.[3] In preparing a course of sermons we come across quotations from authors whose names are only names to us till we read the passages in their contexts. We try to trace, perhaps, the history of Christian controversy, and we find there are whole stretches in the past which, like the Bellman's map, are " a perfect and absolute blank " to us. We are asked about the teaching of some queer sect, such as Anthroposophy, and we have to search out its history and find out what it teaches before we can criticise it.[4] We

---

[1] Cp. my *Immortality* (S.P.C.K., " Little Books on Religion," No. 71).
[2] " To teach is to learn twice." *Pensées*, Titre XIX, " De l'education," 68, p. 245.
[3] Cp. *Modern Churchman*, June, 1944. " God's Foreknowledge and Man's Free Will."
[4] Cp. *Church Times*, April 28, 1944. " The Teaching of Anthroposophy."

are assured by secularist writers that Christianity is a religion of fear and that the Threat of Hell was its " fulcrum " in the Early Church. We are sure that this is untrue, but cannot prove anything till we have read about the martyrs in the Primitive Church, and marked the absence of the element of fear in Early Christian Art and in the history of the Church. In the course of our research we shall note the element of truth that has kept the allegation alive in various forms.[1]

This will educate us in theological proportion and breadth. We shall learn to organise our own " universe " of knowledge by continually adding to our stock of tested fact and putting things into their proper connection with one another. Moreover, it will be a systematisation of things that we have " made our own ". Otherwise we shall be in danger of continuously harping on a few notes. We shall be for ever urging people to " come to Communion ", instead of from time to time going into the whole question of Sacramentalism thoroughly,[2] showing, as Hooker did, its connection with the Incarnation,[3] pointing out its Biblical foundation in the Epistle of St. Paul to the Corinthians, the Synoptists, and the sixth chapter of St. John, or, at another time, giving an outline of its liturgical development, at another considering the attempts of theologians to explain what is meant by the Real Presence, advising on practice to-day, or introducing our hearers to the wealth and beauty of devotional literature in Oriental liturgies, in the Roman Mass, in the Fourth book of A Kempis' *Imitation of Christ*, or in the hymns of Charles Wesley.

Some subjects are continually being mentioned in the pulpit. We are constantly hearing about Confirmation, but the majority of people do not in the least realise what it is. If, however, from time to time we told people about the customs of the Early Church in Baptism and the part played by the Bishop, if at another we pointed out the analogy of admission to full membership in the State on coming of age or the initiation of junior members of Friendly Societies to full adult privileges of their Order, if we elaborated the mutually reinforcing of ideas of the Gift of the Holy Spirit imparted to us in the Laying-on of Hands, and that of the reception into the full life of His activity in the Church, just as in the *Prayer of Humble Access* we pray that Christ may be " in us and we in Him ", if we

---

[1] Cp. my *The Fear of Hell as an Instrument of Conversion* (S.P.C.K., 1939).
[2] Cp. my *Modes of Faith* (S.P.C.K., 1934), Ch. VII, " Sacramentalism," pp. 189–218.
[3] *Ecclesiastical Polity*, Bk. V, Ch. LII–LIV.

explained in detail the why and wherefore of the particular method of preparation adopted in the parish or diocese, then there would be little need to go hunting round only a couple of months before the Bishop comes, trying to persuade reluctant parents, themselves often unconfirmed, to let their boys and girls be " done ", or of saying that coming to classes " need not commit them to anything ", or warning them that they " must not expect to feel any different when it is over ", they would realise what it meant, and come forward of themselves.

On the other hand, some subjects never get treated of in the pulpit at all. They do not fit in anywhere with " the Gospel for the Day ". There is no particular reason why they should be dealt with on one Sunday rather than another. The preacher is not quite sure of himself on the different questions involved, and so they get put off. The single sermon is so difficult to get going. For instance, the whole question of the nature of marriage is left out till there arises some big divorce scandal, and then it is not the time to preach about it. Some sad case of suicide reminds us that though stoicism approved of a man's taking his own life and Japanese tradition applauds it, yet the Almighty has " fixed His canon against self-slaughter ". But it would be cruel to " improve the occasion " just then. The paganism, to say nothing of the waste and bad taste, of our funeral customs does not come into our minds till we have to officiate at the burial of a member of the congregation, and that is precisely the time when it would be unseemly to enlarge upon it in church. So the bad customs go on. Our churchyards are filled with weather-stained white marble crosses and decaying flowers when with the money that is worse than wasted the church itself might have been made beautiful and new churches built more worthy of being offered to God.

To meet the situation is a work of time; therefore the student should begin at once. Naturally he will begin his task with the idea of the Christian Year on his mind, and will be inclined to preach on the Lesson of the Day. He may not know exactly more than a week ahead when he is to preach, and must not begin setting his Vicar right, but even if the work for the week is " arranged on Monday ", he will have a fair idea if he will be expected to preach every Sunday, or, perhaps, only once a month, and it will do him no great harm to be beforehand with his work even if, after all, he is not called upon to go up into the pulpit. His material will probably improve by keeping. If he plans ahead for a twelve-month, a sermon not called for one year will do for its next anniversary.

The scheme for the Christian Year will most obviously follow the lines of the Creed and the Life of Christ and, in Trinity time, of Christian Duty. There will always be opportunities of fitting in single sermons on special subjects that the preacher has made his own.

For instance, he may have studied the structure of a sermon by Phillips Brooks on The Man with Two Talents—the ordinary " man in the street ".[1] This may have come back to him in a slightly different form with the interest centred on the second-class man who feels he can do more than the one-talented man and is disappointed at having to take a second place. What is his function in religion and the Church? What can be said, in the middle part of the sermon, to encourage this man, after calling attention to his case in the introduction? (1) He will not be able to do as much as the ten-talented man, but if he takes his own measure *he will be able to do first-class work on a smaller scale*, if he does not grudge the labour. (2) His work is essential to the whole. We cannot all play first-fiddle, and if we could, and did, there would be no symphony. The player of the tympani who stands and waits for the proper time to play his stroke or roll also serves, *he is essential to the whole orchestra.* (3) The second-class man is the man who is most wanted to-day. We have first-class theologians and many diligent labourers. The spiritual middleman who can take the learned work and make it available for the masses, as the University Extension lecturer brings the University to adult education in the provinces or the schoolmaster who links it up with his boys, is the man we specially need in the Church to-day. As Thomas Fuller said, "The general weight of God's work in the Church lieth on men of middle and moderate parts. That servant who improved his two talents into four did more than the other who increased his five into ten ".[2] And, to conclude, there is nothing degrading in being in the second place. He who was in the form (*i.e.*, had the essential nature) of God thought it not a prize to be grasped at, to be equal with the Father, but became incarnate and lived the life of an artisan for

---

[1] *Twenty Sermons* (Macmillan, 1899), Sermon XI, " The Man with Two Talents," p. 192.

[2] *The History of the University of Cambridge*, Section VI, 10, Caution general. By Thomas Fuller, B.D. A new edition with notes by James Nichols. He continues: " Tradesmen will tell you, it is harder to double a little than to treble a great deal; seeing great banks easily improve themselves, by those advantages which small sums want. And surely many honest (though not so eminent) ministers, who employ all their might in God's service, equal (if not exceed) both in His acceptance and the church's profit, the performances of such who far excel (*sic*) them in abilities."

E

thirty years to bring Life to me. As the little silk-winder sang at
the end of Browning's poem *Pippa Passes* :—

> " All service ranks the same with God,
> With God whose creatures first and last
> Are we, there is no last or first."

If the preacher has had this sermon on the stocks for some time
many other ideas on the subject will have piled up, and another year
he may have ready a sermon on the man with ten talents and on
responsibility *v.* privileges, or, as Phillips Brook himself had, one on
the man with one talent who does not always wrap it up in a napkin.[1]

Thus it would be a good plan to take the *Report of the Commission
on Christian Doctrine*, appointed by the Archbishops of Canterbury
and York in 1927, the result of hard work by many of our leading
theologians, and set out to explain it, knowing there was good
authority behind it.[2] As it stands it is almost unintelligible to the
ordinary man, though I have known it to be taken in part as the
foundation of a set of lectures to deaf and dumb " hearers ". Its
difficulty was evident from the fact that the notice it got in the Press
almost entirely confined itself to two minority details—which it
misunderstood. But to take a few single points—*e.g.*, the Reasons
for Theism, pp. 40–43 (for the Epiphany season), Reason and
Revelation, pp. 44 (for the First Sunday after Trinity), Holy
Scripture and Inspiration, pp. 27–33 (for Bible Sunday, the Second
in Advent), Miracles and the Resurrection, pp. 50–52, 83–88 (for
Eastertide) ; or indeed almost any page might be chosen. As it
stands it is too condensed and in too technical language for the
ordinary reader, but after explaining and illustrating a subject, to
quote its considered and well-balanced words would drive home the
explanation and put it in exact scientific words now become fully
intelligible.

So let us imagine the young preacher coming home from his
holidays. He is the junior member of the staff, and has had to take
them rather late—in September. The months of October, November, and December lie between him and Christmas. He knows he
will have to preach at least twice a month, if not once a week, and
that he may be called upon at seven, or rather six, days' notice to
preach any Sunday. He must plan out a scheme for the whole
quarter, even if he can use only one-half of it.

First of all two dates and one season stand out in his mind.

---

[1] *Sermons by Phillips Brooks* (Dickenson 1885). Sermon VII, p. 134.
[2] S.P.C.K., 1938.

November 1 is All Saints' Day, and is kept with an octave, while probably in October there will be a Harvest Festival for which his Vicar has not been able to find a special preacher. There is also in December the season of Advent, with its four Sundays and Christmas Day to follow.

So he at once thinks of these. For the Harvest Festival he recalls how many of Christ's parables are drawn from agriculture and the light this fact throws on the sights and sounds of those first un-described thirty years of His life,[1] and perhaps he thinks of a sermon on the enduring influences of early life. Or his thoughts turn to the analogies and the contrasts of laws in the natural and in the spiritual world, and a sermon on Natural Science and Religion begins to shape itself. Or perhaps the old arguments for belief in God drawn from the order and design of the world recur to him. For All Saints' Day he may think out what we mean by a saint, and remember Wordsworth's *Happy Warrior*, Kipling's *If*, Newman's picture of a gentleman in his " Idea of a University ", the Chevalier de Méré's ideal of the " honnête homme ", and what the writer of the Epistle to the Hebrews wrote of their " cloud of witnesses " that encom-passed them about; or he thinks of some particular saint, and prepares to get sure of some of the facts in his life or teaching; or he remembers the taunt made that the English Church produces respectable gentlemen but not saints, and asks himself seriously if it is true;[2] and whether perhaps the greatest saints are not those who, like Epaphras, are doing the best work in the world, though all unknown,

> " Men of the plain heroic breed
> That loved Heaven's silence more than fame ";[3]

---

[1] Cp. T. R. Glover, *The Jesus of History* (S.C.M. Press, 1917), Ch. II, " Childhood and Youth," pp. 24–41.

[2] Cp. my *A Church Genuinely Catholic* (S.P.C.K., 1940), Ch. V, " English Catholicism," pp. 114–117.

Cp. Sir Thomas Browne, *Letter to a Friend*: " Be substantially great in thyself, and more than thou appearest to others; and let the world be deceived in thee, as they are in the lights of heaven."

[3] H. R. Lowell, *Under the Willows*, " All Saints," The first verse is:—

> " One feast, of holy days the crest
> I, though no Churchman, love to keep,
> All Saints—the unknown good that rest
> In God's still memory folded deep;
> The bravely dumb that did their deed,
> And scorned to blot it with a name,
> Men of the plain heroic breed,
> That loved Heaven's silence more than fame."

or his thoughts turn to All Souls' Day, and the question of prayer for the dead rises in his mind.

For Advent he thinks of the Four Last Things, but unless he has time to think them over he will only write platitudes about Death, Judgment, Heaven and Hell; if he carries his purpose in his mind for some time he will begin to ask, " What reasons can I give for belief in immortality? ",[1] "What does the resurrection of the body really mean? " " What practical difference does the belief entail? " He will ask himself, "What is judgment? " Is it the decision of an assize, or is it the result of being brought into the presence of what is right? " He may go on to get his mind clear on the question, " What do we mean by heaven? Is it a place or a state? And ' the right hand of God '? Is it not wherever God works and is?[2] Why must we use symbolical language to speak of the world to come? " Or of Hell? We may ask the question, " Is fear a right motive for doing good? Is a thing done from fear of consequences really good

---

Cp. Pascal, *Pensées*, 159: " Les belles actions cachées sont les plus estimables.   Quand j'en vois quelques-unes dans l'histoire, elles me plaisent fort.   Mais enfin elles n'ont pas été tout au fait cachées, puisqu'elles ont été sues ; et quoi-qu'on ait fait ce qu'on a pu pour les cacher, ce peu par où elles ont paru gâte tout ; car c'est là le plus beau, de les avoir voulu cacher." (Fair deeds hidden stand highest in esteem.   When I see them in history they please me much.   But, after all, they were not altogether hidden, since they have been known about, and though men have done their best to conceal them, just this fact that they have been seen spoils all, for the best of all in them was the wish to hide them.)

[1] *Report of Doctrine*, Pt. III, " Eschatology, B., The Future Life: I. Resurrection," pp. 207–211.

[2] Cp. Augustine, *De Civitate Dei*, Bk. XII, Ch. 24, " Manus Dei potentia Dei est qui etiam visibilia invisibiliter operatur."   (The hand of God is the power of God, who works invisibly in the things that we see.)

Clement of Alexandria, *Stromateis*, VI, 16:   " By the finger of God is understood the power of God by which the creation of heaven and earth is accomplished."

Cp. the *Veni Creator*.

Cp. " Tu septiformis munere,
Dextra Dei tu digitus."
(The sevenfold gifts of grace are thine,
O finger of the hand divine.)

The translation is shirked in most English renderings.

Pascal, *Pensées*, No. 687:   " In these expressions we speak of God as men ; and that signifies nothing else than whatever meaning men have in making people sit at their right hand, God has the same.   It is a mark of God's meaning, not of His way of carrying out that meaning."

Cp. my *The Case for Christianity* (Allen & Unwin, 1928), p. 64.

Cp. Thomas à Kempis, *De Imitatione Christi*, Lib. III, cap. 59.   " Ubi tu, ibi coelum ; atque ibi mors et infernus, ubi tu non es."   (Where thou art there is heaven ; and there is death and hell where thou art not.)

or only prudent?[1] Has the threat of Hell ever succeeded?[2]
What is the purpose of punishment? "

Or perhaps he will say, " I must wait for another year. I am
not clear on the subject myself, and will fall back on the topics
suggested by the Prayer Book Calendar. ' What do we mean by
the Coming of Christ? '[3] for Advent Sunday; ' What is Inspiration? ' or ' How did the New Testament come to be written? ' for
Bible Sunday; for the fourth, Ordination Sunday, ' Episcopacy
and the Apostolic Succession? ' "[4] Then perhaps he remembers
that St. Luke's Day comes on October 18, and the opportunity
suggests itself of explaining how the third Evangelist came to write
his Gospel, and the Synoptic Problem and how it shows the many
different channels through which comes our knowledge of Christ's
life; or, it may be, since St. Luke was a doctor, it seems a good
opportunity of showing why Mrs. Eddy and her " Christian Science "
is unscriptural and wrong.

Then perhaps he will feel that all this is rather desultory and
that it would be well to link one sermon with another in his mind
and fill in the gaps from the Beatitudes, at any rate with those of
them round which his ideas have already begun to gather, or with
other single subjects that may have been accumulating ideas in his
thoughts—" How we got the Apostles' Creed," " Baptism in the
Early Church? "[5] and was it by total immersion? " How we got

[1] Cp. J. S. Mackenzie, *A Manual of Ethics* (University Tutorial Press,
6th ed., 1929. Reprinted, 1935), Bk. III, Ch. VI, " Moral Pathology."
§ 5. Punishment, and § 6. Theories of Punishment, pp. 373–376.

[2] Cp. my *The Fear of Hell as an Instrument of Conversion* (S.P.C.K., 1939).

[3] Cp. my *Prediction in the Light of History and Religion* (S.C.M. Press, 1942),
pp. 51–54.

[4] Cp. J. R. Illingworth, *Divine Transcendence* (Murray, 1911), Ch. V. p. 46.
" What does this episcopacy represent? What does it symbolise to the
world?

" For it is, beyond question, a great fact; it looms large in human history
—this order of spiritual rulers that has outlived successive dynasties, itself
instinct, the while, with a vitality that does not age. It is older in England
than the Norman, older than the Saxon, conquest, yet as quick with energy
as ever in the world to-day. It is independent of all forms of political
organisation; independent of all outward conditions of life; whether
called to crown a monarch with the pomp and circumstance of ancient
state, or to live in exile and die in martyrdom among the savage islands of
the sea. It has passed, in its long history, through many a vicissitude, and
seen its days of power and days of persecution; days of reverence and days
of ridicule; dark days, too, at times of degradation from within. But still
through evil report and good report it has persisted."

[5] See my pamphlet with this title (S.P.C.K.), with illustrations showing
that from the earliest times Affusion or pouring was the custom, and not
Total Immersion, and my " Baptism and Christian Archæology " in *Studia*

the Nicene Creed?" and the issue at the Council of 325, "Fate and Free Will"; "How God-Parents originated?" and the duties of sponsorship; "What we can learn from Hymns?" with three worked-out examples; "Rights or Duties," which come first?[1] and then, of course, after Christmas there will be many single points to preach about that are involved in the Incarnation.

Then he makes a rough plan as outlined in Appendix II.

Or he may suddenly be faced with the responsibility of taking charge in some institution or district church where for the next three months he will have to preach twice on Sunday and once on a week-day evening and talk to the children on the Sunday afternoon. At first he is appalled by the thought; then he thinks, "After all, it is less than the ordinary teacher has to do in an elementary school, though he, of course, can repeat his lessons with a new set of boys after a year." So he thinks, "On Sunday mornings I will take the intellectual side of Christianity and go through the articles of the Creed. In the evenings I will try to speak of Christian life and duty, and will follow the lines of the ten commandments or, perhaps, the Duty towards my Neighbour. And on Thursdays I will consider the side where the feelings play a greater part, and will make my subjects those of the Life of Devotion. For the children I can repeat the morning's sermon in simpler form."

Thinking it over, he realises that there are patches in which he has not yet much to say, but he has three months before him, and the gaps will probably fill up as he reads. If they do not he still has time to put in something else. When all is over he will find the experience has been of great value to him in broadening and balancing the whole of his theological outlook.

For a plan, worked out rather more fully after it had been followed in practice, see Appendix III.

At first the middle parts of his sermons will be mainly doctrinal. For this is he already more or less qualified by his College training. He has got at least a very fair outline of dogmatic theology in his preparation for the General Ordination Examination, even if he did not read Theology at the University. He will perhaps feel that giving

---

Biblica (Oxford, 1903), Vol. V, Part iv, p. 239, and Cabrol's *Dictionnaire d'Archéologie et de Liturgie*, Arts "Baptême" and "Baptistère". See also for some of the literary evidence the *Church Quarterly Review* for July, 1914, "Affusion or Submersion?"

[1] Cp. my *The Case for Christianity* (Allen & Unwin, 1928), Ch. I, "The Things that Matter," pp. 31–37, and *Lectures in Hyde Park*, Series III, *Christianity and Conduct* (S.P.C.K., 1929), Lect. I, pp. 11–29.

exhortation and advice to people who are, for the most part, much older and more experienced in life than himself is unseemly, and may be tempted to fall back on the deferential and apologetic manner which, it has been said, cannot declare that we believe, but says, " We all feel, don't we? " But as even a simple lesson given to children in an elementary school about things we all knew before is a pleasure to listen to if the teacher is well trained and can deal clearly with his matter, so a sermon, repeating possibly familiar truths, is never tiresome if the preacher's mind and words are orderly and he has first " made an outline ". In doctrinal sermons the young preacher already speaks with a certain authority on the subjects he has been made to study while his congregation has not.

But he must not neglect sermons of other kinds. He would do well to have at least a mental picture of a scheme of " ascetic " and moral theology. He might, for instance, do worse than take Jeremy Taylor's *Holy Living* to suggest a plan, and speak at different times of Care of our Time, Direction of Intention, the Practice of the Presence of God, of Prayer Private and Common, of Reading or Hearing the Word of God, of Fasting, Prayer, Alms, Repentance, of Preparation for the Holy Sacrament of the Lord's Supper; or of the Moral Duties of Christianity, of Sobriety, Temperance, Chastity, Humility, Modesty and Contentedness, of Christian Justice, of Obedience to our Superiors, of Duty to our Inferiors, of Civil Contracts and Justice in Bargaining, and of Restitution. But in doing so he must not borrow more than headings and must assimilate what is written, leaving it to come up again as his own in his own form, or he will find himself merely quoting the saying of a man who lived in another age and in very different circumstances, so that the phrases he has taken will be dead on his lips.[1]

For the ordering what he has to say of his own he may well take the Beatitudes and the Sermon on the Mount for his framework, first pointing out that the old Ten Commandments were negative, and dwelt mainly on the act, while the Beatitudes are positive, and the Sermon on the Mount goes down to principles and character and motive. He will probably find that certain ideas which recur to him persistently about Christian duty crystallise round one or other of the Beatitudes, while another will seem to attract nothing in particular to itself. Or he may range his thoughts under the

---

[1] Cp. Whateley, *Elements of Rhetoric*, Introduction, § 5 : " He may freely transplant indeed from other writers such thoughts as will take root in the soil of his own mind ; but he must never be tempted to collect *dried specimens.* '

Categories of the four Cardinal Virtues, Temperance, Justice, Prudence, and Fortitude (as Plato and Aristotle did in laying the foundations of Ethics), while adding to them the Christian virtues of Faith, Hope and Charity; but for practical purposes the Ten Commandments still remain for us, for self-examination, for study, for teaching or preaching, the best syllabus of moral theology and casuistry, as they were for Aquinas, when we have made it clear that they must be made positive rather than negative; must be taken in the spirit rather than (as, *e.g.*, in the Fourth Commandment) in the letter; and must be extended to include many similar duties other than those actually mentioned. With very little forcing, as (*e.g.*) by including all duties of honest dealing in things material under the eighth,[1] all sins of the body under the seventh and all duties of truth under the ninth, they can be made to cover all aspects of life.

In a few years the preacher will find he has his whole field of material organised. He will be able to pigeon-hole almost any idea that he feels to belong to his message and store it in its suitable place. Extra notes on subjects already preached about can be filed in the sermons themselves till they are incorporated in a revised or rewritten one. Others will find their place in notes for lessons in school; others in notes accumulating for lectures and discussion classes; others, again, may be incorporated in schemes of books to be written, or, if the book has been written and printed, in its pages to reinforce what has already been published.

All such extracts from his " tab " note-book will have the stamp of his own personality. They will be the things that interest him, the things he has earned the right to say or quote.

For as Amiel wrote:—

> " It is by teaching that we teach ourselves, by relating that we observe, by affirming that we examine, by showing that we look, by writing that we think, by pumping that we draw water into the well." [2]

III

But while the preacher, by taking thought for the morrow, will be organising his theological universe, he must think primarily of his

---

[1] Cp. my chapter on " Honest Dealing " in *The Christian Life*, ed. O. Hardman (S.P.C.K., 1932), Vol. I, pp. 340–370.

[2] Henri Fredéric Amiel, *Fragments d'un Journal Intime*. Précédés d'une étude par Edmond Scherer, 2me ed., Tome I (Paris, 1884), 27 Oct. 1853, p. 82: "C'est en enseignant qu'on s'instruit, en racontant qu'on observe, en affirmant qu'on examine, en montrant qu'on regards, en écrivant qu'on pense, en pompant qu'on fait venir l'eau dans aon puits." Tr. Mrs. Humphry Ward (Macmillan, 1885), p. 79.

hearers. What are they thinking and what do they want to know? How can he best provide them with what they lack?

In the first place, the congregation is made up of individuals. Some are there regularly Sunday after Sunday; others are casual comers-in, and hear a single sermon now and then.

So for the latter each sermon must have a unity and be complete in itself. In open-air preaching such a " casual " may stand and listen for only a few minutes, so, if possible, each period should have something that he can take away with him—some informing story or some telling illustration, some quotation, perhaps, that will stick in his mind. But the regular attendants are the most to be considered, since more can be done with them, and it is through them that ideas permeate to the outside world and by them that the World judges of the Church.

Each sermon, therefore, should be built up on foundations laid beforehand. This, of course, is always done in a series of lectures, but it should be an element in all preaching. These regular church-goers, as well as students beginning their course, should be gradually familiarised with the meaning of theological terms.

When the preacher has to sit in the chancel and listen to someone else in the pulpit he should look at the congregation and mentally put himself in their place. He will see whether they are listening or not. He should say to himself, " Is the preacher using language they understand? Are they taking it in? What should I say if I were preaching on the subject? What subject should I preach upon if I were in his place? What is he assuming that they know when they don't really? " In this way, as Henry Drummond pointed out many years ago in his popular but now almost forgotten book *Natural Law in the Spiritual World*, a dull sermon may be made interesting and, we may add, a lesson may be learned. " There are compensations ", he wrote, " to a flock for a poor minister after all. Where the fare is indifferent those who are really hungry will exert themselves to procure their own supply." [1] Constructive criticism

[1] *Natural Law in the Spiritual World* (Hodder and Stoughton, 2nd ed., 1883), p. 356.
Cp. George Herbert, *The Church Porch*, v. 72.

" Judge not the preacher; for he is thy Judge:
    If thou mislike him, thou conceiv'st him not.
    God calleth preaching folly. Do not grudge
    To pick out treasures from an earthen pot.
        The worst speak something good: if all want sense,
        God takes a text and preacheth patience."

(but it must be constructive) of a dull sermon may be made a useful means of self-education.

So to a preacher in the congregation comes, it may be, the thought, " I could preach a sermon on ' whom not having seen ye love ' "—the idea coming subconsciously afresh into his mind from a passage read in one of Dr. Hensley Henson's books and forgotten for the time being [1]—how it seems to imply that the writer was an eye-witness of Christ's earthly life; how Christ is unique among men in being able to inspire love in men who have never seen Him in the flesh—an affection quite different from sentimentalising about St. Francis and the *Fioretti*, or even from devotion to Christ's mother, which gain what reality they have by reflected light from His person; how this is expressed by the well-known stories of Charles Lamb, and of Napoleon; how it leads to the dilemma *Aut Deus aut homo non bonus*.[2]   And he finds he has more than enough material to sort out and rearrange for a sermon.

Or he is in hospital, and when the chaplain comes and gives his address about " the Church's Calendar and the beginning of the Church's Year ", thinks, " Why doesn't he explain what the seasons actually are and suggest our reading our New Testament from the table of lessons, as so many do—Mr. Gladstone, I believe, did ; and George V used always to ' read his chapter every day '.   And why doesn't he see that we have Testaments in our lockers? "

Or he is in his College chapel at the end of term, and thinks,

[1] H. Hensley Henson, *Christian Morality*, Gifford Lectures (Oxford, 1936), p. 299: " St. Peter, who had seen Jesus and had known Him well, whose love was fed by a thousand personal recollections and who could never lose from memory the form, the face, the manner of his Master, found to his amazement that an affection not less ardent than his burned in the hearts of the multitudes who had never known Jesus by sight nor heard Him speak (I Pet. I, 6–8).   And this has been true ever since of Jesus and of no other person.   The nearest approach has been the devotion of the Roman Church to His mother, which is almost entirely drawn from devotion to Him."

The words are a comment on the question of Dr. Jowett: " Is it possible to feel a personal attachment to Christ such as is presented by Thomas à Kempis?   I think that it is impossible and contrary to human nature that we should be able to concentrate our thoughts on a person scarcely known to us, who lived 1800 years ago."

I had not only read these words, but had actually quoted them in my *The Christian's Claim about Jesus of Nazareth* (S.P.C.K., 1937), p. 123 ; yet the idea came to me as quite original and my own, and I was amazed when I came across the words again and realised where I had got them from.

[2] I have quoted these stories and others in my *Question Time in Hyde Park* (S.P.C.K., 1924), pp. 81, 121.   Dr. Gore's comment on Liddon's use of the dilemma " Either God or a man and not good " will be found there on p. 116.

" I shall probably have to preach next term. I'll tell them not to talk about the ' good old times ', as those tiresome old men did to Ezra when he had begun to rebuild the Temple. Every age has said the same thing—that things aren't what they used to be and religion is dying out. But the world gets steadily better, really— at least, it does if the younger generation keep it up and go forward and do their part. Never be a pessimist, a *laudator temporis acti*." [1]

Or perhaps he has to hear a sermon at a Music Festival, and thinks, " When my turn comes I'm sure they would be interested to hear what part in the whole Liturgy those words play which they will be singing in Bach's B Minor Mass. I must not assume that they know."

Or he may ask himself about his congregation, " What should they have heard and thought about in the course of a year? " And as he is planning his scheme the question will also arise, " What should they hear next year? If at Eastertide I marshal the evidence for the Resurrection of our Lord, and show that the Gospels, while not saying the same things, do not contradict but supplement one another, next year I might consider anti-Christian ' explanations ', like that, *e.g.*, of George Moore in *The Brook Kerith* which that schoolmaster told me the other day one of his colleagues had been reading, and showing why they won't do. Or another year I really ought to go into the question of evidence not growing weaker by lapse of time that Gwatkin's book suggested to me; or, rather, I suppose I should go into the whole question of Miracles, and Hume (what exactly did Hume say?) and Matthew Arnold asserting that ' miracles do not happen '; they are hearing it assumed on every side by writers on Natural Science." [2]

Or he may set himself to collect material for special single sub-jects which get omitted for obvious reasons, like those we mentioned above, such as Funeral Customs, Suicide, and the Marriage Law. Probably none of his Congregation are likely to be attracted by Spiritualism or Christian Science, but very likely they have friends who are. A few may be bitten with British Israelitism or one of the less intelligent forms of Second Adventism, but none, probably, have come across Theosophy in its quasi-Indian form or in its German shape of Anthroposophy, and they have only read about Jehovah's Witnesses in the papers. But in the outside world these movements are often strong, and their adherents many and active. All such subjects require time to prepare and, though it is a temptation, there

[1] See above, p. 16.
[2] Cp. my *The Case for Miracle* (S.P.C.K., 1936).

is little use in attacking them. To attack advertises them and arouses sympathy. The thing to do is to point out how they contradict fundamental principles of Christianity, the belief in immortality, that rests on belief in God, Man's free will, the doctrine of the Cross and the hallowing of suffering and the Incarnation of the Son of God in a material body, the use of reason which God has given us in reading the Bible or judging of the claims to special revelation on the part of Mahatmas. But the blue-pencilling of the minor objections and the stressing of what really matters are a work of time and judgment in preparation.

Then, besides the church-going and sermon-hearing congregation and the people interested in religion, but outside and ignorant of the real nature of Christianity, there is a large public that never comes to church or reads religious books of any sort. These can be effectually reached only at second hand through church-goers, and only through them if they have both the missionary spirit and a sound knowledge of Christian literature. They should be prepared for the work of Christian Evidence and Apologetics. At some time a sermon should be preached on the Christian doctrine of immortality as contrasted with the Indian teaching of reincarnation and Karma, showing how it is unjust (since if you have forgotten all about a previous existence it is practically not you that then existed), and telling of the bad effects the doctrine has, as we are told by people who have lived in India, and who know.[1]

The preacher should listen to the Wireless " Brains Trust " and the questions there put to, or rather chosen by, the Question Master. He should prepare his congregation to be able to answer such questions as " Would it not be better to teach children the chief principles of the great world-religions and leave them to choose for themselves when they get older? " or, " Isn't it unfair to bias a child's mind by religious dogma? " He should read letters in the Press, and he may find one there expressing the interested delight of a young subaltern in the Army who heard a sermon on the historicity of the Gospels and exclaimed, " That is the first time I've heard any one advance a reason for believing the Bible might be true." He should watch the books that are in the Public and Lending Libraries, where he will come across the works of distinguished writers of fiction declaring that in second-century Alexandria Christianity " in all essentials so closely resembled that which was

[1] Cp. E. R. McNeil (Sister Rhoda), *From Theosophy to the Christian Faith* (Mowbray, 1919, new edition with additional matter, October, 1942), pp. 31–33, 94–96.

the outcome of Osiris, Isis and Horus that popular opposition was entirely disarmed ", though he owns that he cannot " find that Bishop Westcott recognises this ".[1]

Or he may watch the active propaganda of the Rationalist Press Association and its cheap, excellently produced selection of standard works of Natural Science, as well as its somewhat reckless and less scholarly attacks on Christianity, and he will find plenty of subjects that will offer him opportunity of giving facts and explaining important truths that will anticipate the Association's propaganda and render it comparatively harmless.

For detailed plans, and for suggestions from Padre's Hour experience, the reader should consult Appendixes IV and V.

But perhaps the greatest opportunities are given in open-air Apologetics. There you meet the serious inquirer, the hostile critic, and the large mass of indifferent men who stand by and listen out of curiosity or to be amused. There in lecturing to them you are able to choose your own subject and to notice their reaction to it. If it does not interest them they go away. There, too, you can hear and answer their questions, both those of the puzzled Christian, of the serious Agnostic, and of the captious objector.

A list of suitable subjects is given in Appendix VIII.

IV

The needs of the world are many and great. There is wide-spread ignorance of religious matters, with a consequent general barrenness of mind that comes from ignoring the existence and educational power of the study of religion. The present-day activity in the school world at which we rejoice gives great occasions for the Church to co-operate. People come to church still in great numbers, and English people still enjoy listening to sermons that they can hear and follow. The Church has special opportunities for " adult education " which no other institution possesses.[2]

Whether she makes use of them all depends on little things—on making notes, on taking time, on power of arrangement and learning to see, on training the ear and tongue, on learning to write, on exercising the imagination to find out what people are thinking about and need to learn.

---

[1] Cp. my *Verify your References* (S.P.C.K., 1938), Ch. XV, " Crescendo," p. 104.

[2] Cp. my *Pastoral Theology and the Modern World* (Oxford, 1920), p. 165: " Christianity the Most Effective Instrument in Education."

IV

THE DELIVERY OF SERMONS

THE PLACE OF SOUND IN THOUGHT

" The first question to receive attention was naturally the one that comes first naturally—how persuasion can be produced from the facts themselves. The second is how to set out these facts in language. A third would be the proper method of delivery; this is a thing that affects the success of a speech greatly; but hitherto the subject has been neglected."

" Our next subject will be style of expression. For it is not enough to know what we ought to say; we must also say it as we ought. Much help is thus afforded towards producing a right impression."—Aristotle, *Rhetoric*, Bk. III, i, 2, 1403b.

" Another thing, very wonderful this learned body (our clergymen) should omit, is learning to read; which is a most necessary part of eloquence in one who is to serve at the altar; for there is no man but must be sensible that the lazy tone and inarticulate sound of our common readers depreciates the most proper form of words that were ever extant in any nation or language, to speak their own wants, or His power from whom we seek relief."—Swift, " Pulpit Eloquence," *The Tatler*, No. 66.

> *Wagner :* " Verzeiht, Ich hör' euch declamiren,
> Ihr las't gewiss ein griechisch Trauerspiel.
> In dieser Kunst möcht'ich was profitieren;
> Denn heut zu Tage wirkt das viel.
> Ich hab' es öfters rühmen hören,
> Ein Komödiant könnt einen Pfarrer lehren."

> *Faust :* " Ja, wenn der Pfarrer ein Komödiant ist;
> Wie das den wohl zu Zeiten kommen mag."

> (" Do I intrude? I heard you, and made sure
> You were declaiming a Greek tragedy.
> Nowadays elocution can secure
> Such power, I seized the opportunity.
> Pardon if I employ a commonplace,
> But a comedian could teach a priest."

> " Yes, if the preacher is a comedian,
> Which, by the way, is no uncommon case."
> —Goethe, *Faust*, tr. G. M. Cookson (Routledge's Broadway Translations, 1927).

WE have now to consider the place of sound in sermon-making. As we saw, it is largely in sight that we think, though seeing is but one element in thought, while sound, and words formed by the movements of pen-holding fingers, form a still more important factor in language.   Speech is the prerogative of man alone in the breathing, or animal, world.[1]

Only one element! There is, as we have seen, a danger in ignoring the element of sight, making what we write and say shapeless, and so failing to be lucid and clear.   There is no less danger in resting in words which may thus become mere words without rhyme or reason.   But, equally, neglect of the importance of sound in speech may easily affect all our thought and action.   The man who pronounces the word " recognise " as " rekernise " will be slipshod in other matters besides pronunciation, and the man who talks with a twang will think with a twang, and read poetry with a twang ; his whole life will become provincial just in so far as he does so, and his appreciation of beauty in prose and poetry will be thwarted and vulgarised.

Equally will the man who hears little, since he reads almost by eye alone, lose what he might have had.   The divorce of poetry from song has gone far to kill the writing of English lyrics, while much modern composition puts forward as poetry what is merely prose arranged in a pattern of print, " displayed " to please the eye of the silent reader, who hears nothing with that inward ear which, no less that the inward eye of which Wordsworth has told us, is " the bliss of solitude ".

English is a language of singular power and beauty of sound. Other tongues have their special qualities and merits.   Clarity of thought and grace of diction are characteristic of French writing. " What is not clear is not French," said Antoine Rivarol, and he knew the merits of his mother-tongue.[2]   But that very clarity has been bought at a price, in that it has lowered French poetry to the

[1] Aristotle, *Politics*, Bk. I, i, 10, 1253a : " Why man is a political animal in a greater measure than any bee or any gregarious animal is clear.   For nature, as we declare, does nothing without purpose ; and man alone of the animals possesses speech.   The mere voice, it is true, can indicate pain and pleasure, and therefore is possessed by other animals as well—but speech is designed to indicate the advantageous and the harmful, and therefore also the right and the wrong ; for it is the special property of man in distinction from the other animals that he alone has perception of good and bad and right and wrong, and the other moral qualities, and it is partnership in these things that makes a household and a city-state."

[2] *Sur l'universalité de la langue française*.   Discours couronné par l'Académie de Berlin en 1784, p. 90, ed. Marcel Hervier (Paris, 1929), p. 90 : " La syntaxe française est incorruptible.   C'est de là que résulte cette admirable clarté, base éternelle de nôtre langue : ce qui n'est pas clair n'est pas français ; ce qui n'est pas clair est encore anglais, italien, grec, ou latin. Pour apprendre les langues à inversions, il suffit de connaître les mots et leur régimes ; pour apprendre la langue française, il faut encore retenir l'arrangement des mots."

(French has a cast-iron syntax.   Hence its marvellous clarity, the eternal

second rank, at least till quite modern times, and has thwarted the
element of suggestion so necessary to poetry of the first order.[1]
The rotundity of full-voiced Italian led to the development of *bel
canto* and made Italy the home of song and opera, but when a group
of Italians get together to talk there is that peculiar clacking sound
which far outdoes that which Miss Matty remembered hearing in
her youth from the old ladies of Cranford.[2]   The force and fullness
of German prose have been invaluable in philosophy, and nearly
every German seems to be able to make an excellent little speech on
the slightest provocation at a *Begrüssungsabend* or an *Abschiedsrede*.
Jane Eyre's cousin, Mary Rivers, was a sound critic when she rolled
out the words, " *Da trat hervor Einer anzusehen wie die Sternen Nacht* ",
and declared, " That is strong. I relish it ",[3] but the German

foundation of our tongue. What is not clear is not French. What is not
clear is still English, Italian, Greek, or Latin. To learn languages that use
inversions in their sentences it is enough to know the words and their cases,
but to learn French you must observe the right order of the words.)

[1] *Ibid.*, p. 91 : " Il est arrivé de là que la langue française a été moins
propre à la musique et aux vers qu'aucune langue ancienne ou moderne :
car ces deux arts vivent de sensations ; la musique surtout, dont la propriété
est de donner de la force à des paroles sans couleur et d'affaiblir les pensées
fortes : preuve incontestable qu'elle est elle-même une langue à part, et
qu'elle repousse tout ce qui veut partager les sensations avec elle."

(The consequence is that French has been less suited for music and
poetry than any other language ancient or modern : for these two arts live
on feelings ; especially music the peculiar character of which is to give force
to words without colour and to weaken strong thoughts, a sure proof that it is
itself a separate language and that it will have nothing to do with anything
that seeks to share its feeling.)

[2] Mrs. Gaskell, *Cranford*, Ch. VI.

[3] Charlotte Brontë, *Jane Eyre*, Ch. XXVIII : " ' Listen, Diana,' said
one of the absorbed students ; ' Franz and old Daniel are together in the
night time, and Franz is telling a dream from which he has awakened in
terror—listen——'   And in a low voice she read something, of which not one
word was intelligible to me ; for it was in an unknown tongue—neither
French nor Latin. Whether it were Greek or German I could not tell.

" ' That is strong,' she said, when she had finished, ' I relish it.' . . .
At a later day I knew the language and the book ; therefore I will here quote
the line : though it was only like a stroke on sounding brass to me : ' Da trat,
etc.' ' Good, good,' she exclaimed, while her dark and deep eye sparkled.
' There you have a dim and mighty archangel fitly set before you. The line is
worth a hundred pages of fustian.' ' Ich wäge die Gedanken in der Schale
meines Zornes und die Werke mit dem Gewichte meines Grimms ' ; I like it.' "

Cp. John Buchan, *Memory Hold-the-door* (Hodder and Stoughton, 1940),
p. 131 : " A man who has been nourished on German metaphysics should
make a point of expressing his thoughts in plain work-a-day English, for the
technical terms of German philosophy seem to have a kind of hypnotic
power ; they create a world remote from common reality where reconcili-
ations and syntheses flow as smoothly and with as little meaning as in an
opiate dream."

language seems to need a Jew like Heine or a genius like Goethe to write, " *Im wunderschönen Monat Mai* " or " *Ueber alle Gipfeln ist Ruh* " and, while the lyrics of Schumann and Schubert are un-surpassed as song, it seems to have proved a disaster to the German peoples to possess such fine national songs as " *Die Wacht am Rhein* " and " *Deutschland, Deutschland über Alles* ", which have done so much in hypnotising a whole people into madness and delusion. But English, soft-spoken, often halting, often mumbled or, by contrast, mouthed, our " beautiful but ill-dressed language ", as Bernard Shaw has called it, by its power of suggestion, by its vagueness, by its lack of precision coupled with its direct and practical structure, has, in spite of its impossible spelling, proved to be the language of poets as well as statesmen, and they not only of the first class—all countries have had *them*—but of a long first-class list as well as of those who are in the second, or even third, but are still " honours men ". So, as Richard Mulcaster said long ago (1530–1611) :—

" Why not all in English, a tung of itself both depe in conceit and frank in deliverie? I do not think that anie language be it whatsoever is better able to utter all arguments either with more pith or greater planesse than our English tung is if the English utterer be as skillful in the matter, which he is to utter, as the foren utterer is." [1]

The best English has been the inheritance of our race in the Liturgy of our Church. Cranmer, when English speech was barely formed, led the way in the Litany and Collects of the *Book of Common Prayer* by producing from the old Latin prayers translations which lost none of their strength and dignity, while far surpassing them in tenderness and beauty. Hooker, who, as Dean Church declared, first showed what English prose might be, translated passages from the Fathers and incorporated them in his *Ecclesiastical Polity* so that you do not notice when he leaves off translating and writes ideas of his own. The Authorised Version of the Bible is universally acknow-ledged to be a model of how our mother-tongue can speak, and it has influenced and inspired later writers while they have worked out other styles of expression, and some people, at any rate, think that

---

[1] *Mulcaster's Elementarie* (1582), edited with an Introduction by E. T. Campignac, at the Clarendon Press, MCMXXV. Cp. 275: " It is our accident which restrains our tung and not the tung it self which will strain with the strongest and stretch to the furthest; for either government if we were conquerers, or for cunning, if we were treasurers, not anie whit behind either the subtile *Greeks* for couching close, or the statelie *Latin* for spreding fair. Our tung is capable, if our people would be painful."

F

the Revised Version of 1884 has even surpassed it by restoring the beauty of accurate thought while seldom destroying the felicities of sound that the Authorised Version has made familiar to us all.[1]

Yet we hear continual complaints about reading and preaching in church. It is no new thing. Hooker complained of the " irksome deformities " of " endless and senseless effusions of indigested prayers ",[2] and the Puritans of his day objected to the " confused noise of the people one speaking after another " in saying their responses.[3] George Herbert warned the " Countrey Parson " that the people should not say their part in " a huddling or slubbering fashion ",[4] and Isaak Walton deprecated what he called the " muddling up " of the prayers on the part of the priest. Sheridan wrote his *Art of Reading* for the guidance of the clergy in church with a " peculiar set of marks " to guide their pronunciation,[5] while writer after writer has written on the subject in lectures to the clergy,

[1] Hooker, *Ecclesiastical Polity*, Bk. I (Oxford, 1896), ed. R. W. Church, Introduction, p. xix: " It first revealed to the nation what English prose might be; its power of grappling with difficult conceptions and subtle reasonings, of bringing imagination and passion to animate and illuminate severe thought, of suiting itself to the immense variety of lights and moods and feelings which really surround and accompany the work of the mind; its powers of attracting and charming like poetry, its capacity for a most delicate or most lofty music."
     Cp. *The Dictionary of National Biography*, Vol. XI (Oxford, 1937–1938), p. 1113. Art. " Lightfoot, Joseph Barber," by F. J. A. H(ort): " In after years, when the outcry against the Revised New Testament was loudest, he remained faithful to his original contention, and expressed publicly his dissent from most of the objections made, which he believed to originate chiefly in the unrecognised operations of mere familiarity." (Charge of 1882, pp. 77–81, and elsewhere.)
     [2] *Ecclesiastical Polity*, Bk. V, Ch. xxv, § 5: " The irksome deformities whereby through endless and senseless effusions of indigested prayers they oftentimes disgrace in most unsufferable manner the worthiest part of Christian duty towards God, who herein are subject to no certain order, but pray both what and how they list."
     [3] *Ibid.*, Ch. (xxxvi, § 1), Note from Cartwright.
     [4] *The Priest to the Temple, or The Countrey Parson*, Ch. VI.
     [5] Cp. Whately, *Elements of Rhetoric*, Part IV, " Of Elocution," Ch. ii, § 2, and Appendix N for examples.
     This work, however, was criticised by Richard Cull, Tutor in Elocution, in his " *Garrick's Mode of Reading the Liturgy of the Church of England*. A new Edition, with a preliminary Discourse by Richard Cull, Tutor in Elocution " (London and Cambridge, 1840). In the original Preface of 1797 he wrote: " Mr. Sheridan in his *Lectures on Reading*, aiming at ' rendering the Clergy more *correct* than *fervent* in this part of their duty ' has not ' endeavoured to teach them the manner in which the service might be read with that *glow* of animated devotional piety, befitting its sacred importance, and from which the people would receive the highest advantages (*sic*) through the medium of sympathy and example '." A specimen of Garrick's Mode will be found below, p. 72.

and bishop after bishop has in his charges chid his hearers for their faulty elocution. Laymen have written innumerable letters to the papers and have made speeches at Church Congresses, giving excellent advice which has failed to reach its mark owing to cries from the body of the hall of, " Speak up, sir. We can't hear." [1]

There has been much criticism but little suggestion of remedies beyond vague advice to " speak naturally "—advice which, followed on the stage, results in inaudibility [2]) ; or definitely wrong suggestions have been proffered about " emphasising your little words ", which often quite alters their meaning; about " pronouncing your consonants ", which are often omitted in correct speech of the educated ; [3] and on " not dropping your voice at the end of the sentence ", without explaining whether dropping it in pitch is meant (which is right), or dropping it in force (which is wrong).

The great mass of such critics do not, in the advice they give, realise that sound is an element in all thought, that human speech is an art the rules of which have been carefully studied in the science of phonetics, and that elocution or speech-training is an art, though in many places there are no means of getting the special guidance that is necessary. It is an essential preliminary to rhetoric, though there are seldom any opportunities of getting it taught thoroughly. Continual complaints are made that " it is not taught in our Theological Colleges ", and it must be owned that the " practice in reading and preaching " gained there is seldom adequate, and may often become merely a means of confirmation in bad habits, though

[1] *The Times*, September 9, 1933, " Audibility." At a meeting of the General Committee of *The British Association* a member made the plaintive suggestion to the President that something should be done to make speakers more audible to their hearers. There is no exact record as to whether or not the wisdom of the Association suggested a suitable remedy, for unfortunately it happened that the question was audible to few of those present and the reply to fewer.

[2] Cp. Louis Calvert, *Problems of the Actor* (Simpkin, Marshall, 1919), p. 43 : " The beginner is often told by the director not to strain and shout, but to ' speak naturally ', and then when he does speak naturally, he is told that he cannot be heard. This is a baffling paradox, and one which everyone who takes up stage work is likely to meet sooner or later. As a matter of fact, the natural speaking voice is of little or no use on the stage, and neither is the shout. The secret of it is that a man should so train his voice that he has the range and the pitch that is necessary, but also the technique and the control which enable him to seem to speak naturally."

[3] In an old number of *Punch* a Duchess's companion was represented as saying, " O, yes, Duchess. I saw Her with Her Habitual Hypocrisy, Holding His Hand as He was Haranguing in the old Hotel Hall." To which the Duchess replied, " Good gracious, child. Don't go stickin' in your ' h 's like that, or people will think your ancestors dropped them and that you're pickin' 'em up again."

the critic seldom seems to have tried to find out what is actually being done in the institutions he criticises. So it seems that the clergy must for the most part teach themselves, and it is hoped that the following suggestions, based very largely on what we tried to do at King's College in the University of London, may prove useful. After all, self-instruction is the surest teaching.

I

Let us, then, first consider speech as a mode of thought. It is difficult to do this in writing, since so much that is to be said by way of illustration should be said by the living voice, *viva voce*. Our meaning is so often expressed by accent, tone, and phrasing. By change of accent that meaning can be entirely altered. As has been pointed out, the words "Are—you—going—to—London—to—morrow?" can be made to mean five different things, according as each word is stressed or not. "*Are* you going, etc.?" I thought you had given up the idea. "Are *you* going, etc.?" I thought someone else was making the journey. "Are you *going*?" I thought you were coming from Town. "Are you going to *London*?" I thought you had settled to go to Oxford. "Are you going to London *to-morrow*?" I hoped you were staying some time longer. But it is difficult to express this in print.

Whately in his *Elements of Rhetoric*, " designed principally for the instruction of unpractised writers ", points out that the words " And there was light " may be taken in more than one sense, and his work seems to be the source of the oft-repeated story of the bishop who made his ordinands read aloud the first chapter of the book of Genesis the day before their ordination—a singularly useless proceeding, as you cannot begin to teach a man how to read intelligently at the last minute. It only distresses him to catch him out and to find fault; he should have been trained to express himself properly long before. It may mean " and light appeared ", as described by Milton and set to music by Haydn; if the word " was " is stressed with a rising intonation, that light already existed and that the Almighty made a quite superfluous command; or it may express wonder and awe at the majesty of His creation of light out of darkness. As Whately writes:—

" Here we can indicate indeed to the eye that the stress is to be upon ' *was* ', but it may be pronounced in different tones; one of which would alter the sense, by implying that there WAS light ALREADY." [1]

[1] *Elements of Rhetoric*, Part IV, Ch. I, § 3 note.

Or, to take a third example. In the Nicene Creed we express our belief that Jesus of Nazareth was " God *of* God, Light *of* Light. Very God *of* Very God ". The Greek behind is Θεον Ἐκ Θεοῦ, God *from* God, φῶς Ἐκ φωτός, Light *from* Light, Θεον ἀληθινον Ἐκ Θεοῦ ἀληθινοῦ, Very God *from* Very God ". The words were introduced to rule out the teaching of Arius, who said, " There was a time when He was not ", that the Son was not eternally begotten, but was created in Time. The whole meaning is lost unless the preposition " of " is stressed. " God of God " means nothing.

Again, the implication of a sentence can be entirely changed by the tone with which it is uttered. As Albert Chevalier explained in one of his Cockney coster-songs, " It ain't so much the things 'e says as the narsty wy 'e says it." Wordsworth's lines about Lucy are full of tragic pathos when rightly spoken; but if uttered with a sigh of relief an entirely different impression is conveyed by the couplet:—

> " But she is in her grave, and Oh
> The difference to me! " [1]

So by different phrasing the meaning of a sentence can be entirely altered in its effect. The same words, " I don't agree with you ", can be made provocative or conciliatory, according to the tone by which they are uttered. Socrates saw that the Demagogue would " hire men with fine, loud, persuasive voices to advocate his principles and to draw over the commonwealth to tyranny and democracy ",[2] and Mr. Graham Wallas has severely criticised the training of men in salesmanship to persuade people to buy things they do not want. There is a story of an actress who, in training her pupils for the stage, kept them practising for months on the single word " Oh ", till they could express the whole range of emotion through surprise, fear, exultation, grief, doubt, hesitation, disappointment, remonstrance, etc., etc., whereas M. Jourdain, when asked what he did when he made the same exclamation, merely said, " I just say Oh "—" *Mais je dis, O !* " [3]

A power of control over the accents and tones of the voice is necessary for the interpretation of poetry to bring out all its resources of meaning. So much might be done in the pulpit to bring home its message by illustrations from verse. So much harm may be

---

[1] Wordsworth, " She dwelt among the untrodden ways."
[2] *Republic*, Bk. VIII, 568.
[3] Molière, *Le Bourgeois Gentilhomme*:
> " Qu'est ce que vous faites quand vous prononcez, O?
> Mais je dis, O."

brought about by false interpretation of words used in prayer.
When Boswell asked Mr. Walker if he had taught many of the
clergy,[1] Dr. Johnson ejaculated, " I hope not ", but speech-training
need not necessarily follow the lines of *Garrick's Mode of Reading the
Liturgy.* He, we are told, recommended after reading the opening
sentence at Morning Prayer,

> " a look, expressive of the utmost SUITABLE GRAVITY, to be cast
> slowly around the congregation, the voice rather LOW, and
> denoting, together with the whole manner, that SOLEMN and
> REVERENTIAL RESPECT which is due to the place of worship,
> DEARLY BELOVED BRETHREN.
>
> " Here make a pause much longer than the comma, or
> indeed, than the time which is thought necessary after a semi-
> colon—then proceed with a SOLEMN DIGNITY of tone, and
> with a TENOR of SMOOTH REGULAR delivery." [2]

Fancy this every Sunday for a year!

The first step to be taken in learning right delivery is to arouse
interest in the whole subject; for with interest we begin to be critical.
We start listening to others, and to ourselves. The student has to
be persuaded that it is quite possible for him to speak and read well.
He has to get over self-consciousness and the feeling that he is doing
something unnatural, or even absurd, when he speaks or reads with
expression. He has to learn to take pleasure in the right use of his
voice, to realise that good diction is an art, and an art within his
reach.

How this may be done is, perhaps, best learned by describing the
method used in one school.   If it only calls forth criticism it may form
a foundation for a better way, and may at least give suggestions for
self-training on similar, or better, lines.

At King's College, London, we had a three years' course in the
Theological Faculty for those seeking the Associateship as a quali-

---

[1] *Life of Dr. Johnson,* April 18, 1783, Oxford ed., Vol. IV, p. 206:
" Mr. Walker, the celebrated master of elocution, came in, and we went
upstairs into the study. I asked him if he had taught many clergymen.
Johnson: ' I hope not.' Walker: ' I have only taught one and he is the
best reader I have ever heard, not by my teaching, but by his own natural
talents.' Johnson. ' Were he the best reader in the world I would not
have it told that he was taught.' Here was one of his peculiar prejudices."
[2] *Op. cit.,* p. 68, see note 5. " So it goes on. ' I pray and beseech you '
is to be said ' in rather a *fervent supplicating* tone and look '. At ' as many as
are here at present ' he is told to ' look gently around your congregation '
and to say the words ' the throne of heavenly grace' with a look *upwards* of
great *reverence* and with a suitable tone."

, but it is doubtful s".)
Incidentally, these will also prove useful for choir-boys later on.
[2] Many other examples for practice can be found in W. Ripman's
The Sounds of Spoken English (Dent, 13th ed., 1926) (a revised version under
the title *English Phonetics*, 1934), an invaluable book for the practical study
of phonetics, *e.g.* :

A tell-tale tattling termagant that troubled all the town.
Loudly and long little Lily laughed.
She stood at the door of Burgess's fish sauce shop, welcoming him in.
Were you aware where we were when we were at the weir?
A library literally littered with contemporary literature.
The moan of doves in immemorial elms.
And murmuring of innumerable bees.

of phonetics in common use by teachers of foreign languages in schools, though strangely ignored by singers and choir-trainers, which they, too, might find useful in training church choirs. But chiefly the object was to *make them mouth-conscious*.

The remainder of the hour was spent in the actual practice of reading. This was done over secular literature, since in using it for such a purpose you can correct faults more freely, you can joke, you can parody by exaggeration, you can illustrate by imitation, you can make people use their voices in all sorts of different ways that would be profane in reading the Bible.

We used the *Golden Treasury* as a text-book, and confined ourselves to poetry mainly because it gives more scope for varied expression and provides more variety—dramatic, narrative, lyric, and meditative.[1]   But chiefly our aim was to learn to interpret the

---

[1] We began generally with Wordsworth.
O friend, I know not.
Milton, thou should'st be living at this hour.
Ode to duty.   (Rather too difficult for a beginner.)
Ethereal minstrel.
O blithe new-comer.
Earth hath not anything,
Behold her single in the field.
I wandered lonely as a cloud.
Tax not the royal saint.
Then we went on to Tennyson.
Break, break, break.
Tears, idle tears.
Then back to Shakespeare's sonnets.
When I have seen.
Since brass nor stone.
That time of year thou may'st in me behold.
Then to Shirley.
The glories of our blood and state.
To George Herbert.
When God at first made man.
Then to Milton.
When I consider how my life is spent.
Blest pair of sirens.
To Shelley.
I met a traveller.
To Keats.
Season of mist and mellow fruitfulness.
(Rather too difficult.)
To Browning (for dramatic pieces).
Oh, to be in England.
Prospice.
The Lost Leader.
Nobly, nobly Cape St. Vincent.

meaning of what we read and to feel its beauty, to let ourselves go, and to get over shyness and self-consciousness by the ordeal of reading before a class from a desk, and that a class of fellow students. Each piece was read by two or three in turn to give all a chance of trying and of criticising different renderings. Except that he lacks a critical audience, any young preacher can try this method for himself.

At the end of the year we had a competition in which the students voted a small prize to the reader they thought the best. The results in class during the term had often been quite good; the result of the competition was invariably disappointing. The reading was either lifeless or melodramatic. The votes nearly always went to a vigorous speaker who did nearly all the wrong things. But the test *had set them all listening and thinking*.

II

They had got the idea that speech is an art,[1] and the listening and thinking went on all through the second year subconsciously. In the chapel services day by day we heard the lessons read, and felt how the readers conveyed, or failed to convey, their meaning. Reading in chapel was never criticised by the staff except on matters of fact, as to whether it was too soft or unnecessarily loud. The service was not to be turned into an elocution lesson. If mistakes were made, they were not commented on; the readers were to think of what they were reading, and not of themselves. But we learned to use our voices in quiet, careful, and reverent speech, in saying the Psalms together on the low, natural note of the speaking voice. In the music hour, once a week, we learned to sing, and sing in tune without shouting or straining, hymns unaccompanied and transposed down so that we could use our voices naturally and quietly, phrasing them according to their meaning,[2] learning the elements of sight-reading from books with tunes, over unison singing in which the good readers helped those who knew less, and day in,

---

To Christina Rossetti.
  Does the road wind uphill all the way?
And Clough.
  Say not the struggle naught availeth.
  Where lies the land?
et cetera.
  [1] Cp. Bertrand Russell, *Let the People Think*, p. 83: " The conception of speech as something capable of aesthetic value is dying out."
  [2] Cp. *Church Times*, November 28, 1941, " Melodious Intelligence ". See Appendix I, pp. 86–88.

day out, were accustomed to speak and sing reverently and sincerely in our worship. Some learned, too, a great deal in the College Musical and Dramatic Societies. A male-voice choir of a few, more skilled, musicians, accustomed to watch a conductor, was of great use in keeping the singing in chapel on right lines, especially when dispersed among the whole body at times when the building was full, at the beginning and end of the Term.

But especially in the art of conversation, and perhaps in listening to, or criticising, our lecturers, we learned to talk better, to speak more clearly, and to develop voices " soft, gentle, and low ", which, as King Lear said of Cordelia, is " an excellent thing in woman " [1] and no less so in man. Aristotle, among other traits generally attributed to the " high-minded man ", mentioned " a slow gait, a deep voice, and a deliberate utterance ".[2]

The difference was noticeable in the final year, and then we began to study speech as an art, and the actual use of the voice for the special needs of our profession in the pulpit, prayer-desk, and the Altar. We had the use of a large hall, and there, again, avoiding biblical passages, we began practice with Shakespeare. *Pace* Demosthenes; this was better than the open air, which demands special methods for its special conditions. Nor did we, as he did, find it necessary to go to the seaside or to put pebbles in our mouths to correct ourselves of " robicosity " [3] and learn to pronounce our

---

[1] *King Lear*, Act. V, Sc. iii, 274.

[2] *Eth. Nic.*, IV, iii, § 34. The whole passage runs: " Other traits generally attributed to the great-souled man are a slow gait, a deep voice, and a deliberate utterance; to speak in shrill tones and to walk fast denotes an excitable nervous temperament, which does not belong to one who cares for few things and thinks nothing great."

So Cicero, *Orator*, XVII, 56, wrote: " Therefore one who seeks supremacy in eloquence will strive to speak intensely with a vehement tone, and gently with lowered voice, and to show dignity in a deep voice and wretchedness by a plaintive tone. For the voice possesses a marvellous quality, so that from merely three registers, high, low, and intermediate, it produces such a rich and pleasing variety in song."

Cp. Boswell's *Life of Dr. Johnson*, April 18, 1783, Oxford Edition, Vol. IV, p. 207. " Johnson: ' He [Sheridan] reads well but he reads low; and you know it is much easier to read low than to read high, for when you read high, you are much more limited, your loudest note can be but one, and so the variety is less in proportion to the loudness. Now some people have occasion to speak to an extensive audience, and must speak loud to be heard.' Walker: ' The art is to read strong though low.' "

[3] Cp. Diogenes Laertius, *Euclides of Eubulides* II, 108: " Demosthenes was probably his pupil and thereby improved his faulty pronunciation of the letter " r ".

Liddell and Scott. ῥωβικός, " unable to pronounce ῥῶ."

" r "s. Most of us had learned at least the way to do so in the first year.

Dramatic pieces were chosen. An hour was just enough for five to try each piece while the other four made the " house ". We frankly " ragged " and burlesqued them, overdoing it to learn to let ourselves go, to shout without altering the quality of our vowels, to over-articulate our consonants without changing them, to extend our range of pitch, to use the lower registers of our voice, only rising to the higher when the meaning demanded it, not to accent un-accented words, to use our knowledge of phonetics in details, to associate different tones with variety of pathos, to get a musical quality into our diction, to stand and face an audience, to learn the elements of associating voice with gesture,[1] so that, if in our nature, they might reinforce one another later on, in order that, by our learning to do all these things consciously and by effort, they might become natural and spontaneous when we were serious in church and wanted to think only of the meaning of what we were trying to express.

The pieces chosen were generally :—

(1) Hamlet's " Speech to the Players " (Act II, Sc. ii), as embodying the principles of good dramatic speech, and the wrong of over-doing it, which we were for the time deliberately doing for

[1] Cp. Cicero, *Orator*, XVII, 55, tr. H. M. Hubbill (Loeb Library, " Manner of Speech (Quomodo autem dicatur) falls into two sections, delivery (actio) and use of language. For delivery is a sort of language of the body, since it consists of movement or gesture as well as of voice or speech."

56 : " Demosthenes was right, therefore, in considering delivery to be the first, second and third in importance."

Cp. *Brutus*, 142, tr. G. L. Hendrikson (Loeb Library): " You can see by his [Antonius'] example how all this bears out the truth of the dictum attributed to Demosthenes; who was asked what was first in oratory? and replied to his questioner ' action '. What was second ? ' action ', and again third, ' action '. Nothing else so penetrates the mind, shapes, moulds, turns it, and causes the orator to seem such a man as he wills to seem."

Note.—The Latin " action " (ὑπόκρισις) seems to render the saying of Demosthenes more effectively than our more precise equivalent "delivery". We have preserved the Latin usage in " actor ".

Dr. Johnson says of Watts (*Lives of the Poets*) that " he did not endeavour to assist his eloquence by gesticulation, for, as no corporeal actions have any correspondence with theological truth, he did not see how they could enforce it ", though he himself, " at the conclusion of weighty sentences ", " gave time, by a short pause, for the proper impression ". By the " James-Lange theory " that bodily expression creates feeling and influences character, it would seem to be an essential part of oratory, though in Englishmen it is restrained where Southern races gesticulate. Still, even when singing in English a good singer sings with his whole body, even if only by keeping it still, and bodily motion, whether expressed or restrained, seems to be an integral factor in thought.

practice in learning what to avoid; and the " coming tardy off ", which we were trying by that means to overcome, and so to learn change and variety.

(2) " Clarence's Dream " (*Richard III*, Act I, Sc. iv), to learn to let ourselves go and to simulate weariness, surprise, horror, agony of body and mind, revenge, hatred, exhaustion, all in one speech, by rapid passing from one to the other, ending perhaps with the beauty of calm reflection in the words

" Sorrow breaks seasons and reposing hours, etc."

(3) *Julius Caesar*, " Brutus and Cassius " (Act I, Sc. ii), with two readers playing up to one another antiphonally, with persuasion, by suggestion, in cumulative appeal, and contempt, in the denigration of Caesar.

(4) " The Quarrel Scene of Brutus and Cassius " (Act III, Sc. ii, 7) for the rousing of anger and its appeasement, appeal to emotion, the assumption of sorrow, generous forgiveness and the sealing of friendship, adding (if the reading was getting more sincere), as a passage of sheer beauty of words and feeling, the parting scene beginning " The gods to-day stand friendly ", in Act V, Sc. i, l. 94.

And finally (5) Brutus' " Speech to the Citizens ", followed by Mark Antony's " Friends, Romans, Countrymen " (Act II, Sc. ii, l. 79) for a sustained crescendo of appeal, playing on the passions of an audience with all the tricks of popular oratory.

The shortness of an academic term and the limitations in times imposed by the necessity of dealing with large numbers in sets of five, limited the programme, but the self-teacher could easily make out a longer one from the works of Shakespeare.

In all this we were able to use our elementary knowledge of phonetics in detail so as to preserve normal pronunciation in conversation, or reading in a room, from being distorted by the changed conditions of a hall.   This secures what is called a " natural voice ", by which is meant a highly artificial one, which sounds quite natural in the unnatural conditions of a theatre or church.   For this it is necessary to be careful that you do not distort your vowel sounds and, for instance, say " Chroist " for " Christ ".   But instead of practising on our Saviour's title, you take a word with the same vowel, such as " life ", and instead of saying, " Don't pronounce it as ' loife ' ", you say, " Bring your tongue a little more forward and un-round your lips.   Open your mouth a little wider from side to side. Don't you hear the difference?   Now do it again and see if you can't feel the change in the position of your tongue and your lips."

You can teach a man not to stress unaccented syllables, not by imitating his wrong pronunciation, which he will at once deny is like his own, but by reminding him that every unaccented vowel in English becomes either " er " (the sign in phonetic script is an inverted " e ") as in the last syllable of " never ", or " i " as in that of " very ", or " O " as in that of " window ". You can correct the false pronunciation of words like " fear " and " near ", which singers justify and pronounce as " fee-rr " and " nee-rr ". And, indeed, it is quite correct in Scotch, and is characteristic of Cockney speech, but is unsuitable for the pulpit in England. Broadcasting announcers know exactly how such sounds are framed, yet I have heard a conductor of a famous choir tell its members to pronounce a word more like two quite different ones, the first of which demanded the bringing of the tongue more forward and the second the drawing it farther back ! [1]

III

So the speech learned in the classroom and in the hall as a science could be practised, without further thought of its mechanism, in church. When we had learned in some degree to control our voices while letting ourselves go, we went into the chapel to try the adapting of our knowledge to special uses in the various parts of public worship.

First we went up into the pulpit. There we read an introduction of a sermon by some great preacher. The five we used were Phillips Brooks' *Make the Men Sit Down*; Liddon's *Christ in the Storm*; F. W. Robertson's *Triumph over Hindrances—Zaccheus*, or his *Christ's Judgment Concerning Inheritance*; and Newman's *The Religious Use of Excited Feelings*. We noticed that the sermons were generally of three or four paragraphs, though not always printed so; how they started with what the congregation already knew, but reminded them of it, so as to lead their thoughts up to a point; how this was done either by working up to it, or by starting with it and expanding it to form a background for what was to follow; and, after reading it over to ourselves, we tried to see how far we could bring out the chain of thought by the various tones in which we read the different sections. We began by making sure that the desk was at the right height and the light sufficient, and then giving out the text, looking straight at

[1] Cp. Walter Ripman, *The Sounds of Spoken English* (Dent, 13th ed., 1926), 38, 2, p. 73: " The dull vowel (ə) occurs very commonly in ordinary speech; most unstressed syllables contain this vowel or the variety (i) mentioned below. It is found, for instance, in the italicised syllables of vow*el*, var*i*ety, ord*i*n*a*ry." In fuller detail in *English Phonetics* (1934), pp. 137–141.

the congregation of five, and not hurrying on till they had had time to take it in and were ready to listen. The centre of interest was in them and in the man farthest away at the back. We tried to put our own personal interpretation into the words, giving them force, not by declaiming them as in the hall during the term before, but by the restraint that gives the sense of force.

The next week we went to the lectern and read from the Bible. Now we were reading not *to*, but *with* (except for the four others in the class), the imaginary congregation. The centre of interest was now in the book before us. We were to interpret Isaiah, St. Paul, or the writer of the Apocalypse, though, of course, with care that we did it in such a way that all, even those farthest off, could hear and follow *with* us in our interpretation. We tried to realise, and to feel, that reading is an art as much as singing is an art, and that the public honouring of God in church demands the offering of our best in speech quite as much as in song. Like the Jongleur de Nôtre Dame, who being unable to play or sing went by night into the monastery church, to the horror of the watching monks, there before the statue of our Lady performed all the very best juggling tricks in his repertoire, so we tried to practise the art of reading aloud *ad majorem Dei gloriam.*

The next week we went on to the saying of the service. Now the centre of interest was to be in One above. Sinking their individual peculiarities, priest and people unite to adore Him. There must be no preaching of the prayers to the people, no peculiarities of manner in which they cannot join, no casual tones of conversation. There must be in the priest's mind now the thought of uniting with the congregation in Common Prayer. Self must be sunk in the whole worshipping body. The voice should be like beautiful, impersonal, clear print. The words should be audible without strain, perhaps a little over-articulated and slightly over-emphasised on each recurring stress of English phrasing, always so that attention is attracted to the matter, and not to the speaker. The pitch should be low—just that of the natural note of the ordinary man's voice when speaking quietly with others. If you listen, the ordinary " buzz of conversation " is on about B flat, the second line from the bottom on the base clef, or even lower. Familiar words may be said a little faster, as the mind travels more rapidly with them, but not too faintly or too fast for all to join in mentally or with the voice. In united responsive prayers time must be left for movements of the body, for rising from the knees or turning to the East. We practised saying the Commandments (in the shortened form of the 1928 Prayer Book) from the

chancel (not actually from the Altar), and listening for the last words
of the Kyries, not as said by a server close by, but taking our cue
from the last sound from the people at the farther end of the church,
lest we should cut in too soon with the next, and keeping our voices
still even and up, so that they could come in with their part in the
Amen at the end of each prayer.

Then, the next week, we formalised the natural music of the
spoken voice in the sung service. The natural note of the voice at
the end of the first Lord's Prayer at Matins was taken for the first
note of praise and worship beginning with " Oh Lord, open thou
our lips ", so that there was the least possible contrast between the
two. Just as at Alexandria, Athanasius, so Augustine tells us,[1] made
the reader sing " *tam modico vocis inflectione ut pronuntianti vicinior esset
quam canenti* ". After practising speaking musically, we practised
singing that should retain and interpret clearly the meaning of the
words in the simple inflexions of versicles and responses and in the
singing of the Litany in the natural rhythm of spoken phrases.

Then, for those who were " musical "—and eighty per cent.
proved to be so, though some ten per cent. had not their vocal
muscles under control and could not keep in tune, and some ten
per cent. had been told in their youth not to sing as they were
" tone-deaf ", and so had never tried to correlate what they heard
with the sounds that they made—we practised the intonations of the
Creed and Gloria, the musical rendering of the Proper Prefaces and,
if we wished, the chanting of the Epistle and Gospel in natural
speech rhythm, and we had among us those who could sing solo,
both recitative and arias, from oratorio.

Thus we went through the whole range of musical voice-
expression in thought, if not in sufficient practice. We considered,
for instance, the different ways in which such words as those of
which Walter Pater [2] said :—

[1] *Confessions*, Bk. X, Ch. xxxiii, 50: " That seems to me the safer way
which I remember has often been told me of Athanasius the Bishop of
Alexandria, who made the reader of the psalms chant with just that slight
inflexion of the voice that he seemed more like one speaking than singing."
(" Tutiusque mihi videtur quod de Alexandrino episcopo Athanasio saepe
mihi dictum commemini, qui tam modico flexu vocis faciebat sonare
lectorem psalmi, ut pronuncianti vicinior esset quam canenti." Quoted
from Rabanus Maurus, *De Inst. Cleric*, by Hooker, *Eccles. Polit.*, Bk. V, ch.
xxxviii, 3. He in turn seems to have quoted it from Isidore of Seville, *De
Eccl. Off.*, 1, v, 2.)
[2] Cp. my *The Christian's Claim about Jesus of Nazareth* (S.P.C.K., 1937),
p. 56: " Mrs. Humphry Ward, the gifted author of *Robert Elsmere*, wrote in
her book, *A Writer's Recollections*, how in her ' ardent years of exploration and

"There are such mysterious things. Take that saying, 'Come unto me all ye that are weary and heavy laden'. How can you explain that? There is a mystery in it. Something supernatural."

How it could be quoted in conversation,[1] how given out as a text from the pulpit, how it should be rendered in the reading of the Second Lesson, how it should be said liturgically in the Comfortable Words at the Altar, how, if the strict ceremonialist experts allow it, it might be sung there (as it used to be in the old " ritualist " days), how it might be chanted in the Gospel, how it might be rendered as an antiphon by one or by several voices in free rhythm or contrapuntal harmony, how it might have been used as a recitative in oratorio, how it was set as an aria in strict barred time and orchestral accompaniment by Handel in *The Messiah*.

IV

I criticised above the ordinary type of book on homiletics, but when the student has left college and is preaching in the parish such books gain a certain value, if only in keeping alive the interest of the preacher in his art. It is worth while to study the sermons of great preachers of the past, though the conditions of their times were so different that they have to be " translated " into the terms of to-day. But it is singular how few sermons have found any enduring place in literature, and where men like Chrysostom, Augustine, Donne, Bossuet, Jeremy Taylor or Newman have found their place, in most cases their greater title to fame is found in their other works. A book like Canon Charles Smyth's *The Art of Preaching* [2]

---

revolt ' she met the great art critic Walter Pater, and ' reckoning confidently on his sympathy and with the intolerance and certainty of youth ' said that ' orthodoxy could not possibly maintain itself long against its assailants, especially in the historical and literary camps, and that we should live to see it break down '. ' He shook his head ', she tells us, ' and looked rather troubled.' ' I don't think so,' he said. Then with hesitation: ' And we don't altogether agree. You say it is all so plain. But I can't. There are such mysterious things. Take that saying, ' Come unto me all ye that are weary and heavy laden! How can you explain that? There is a mystery in it, something supernatural.' "

[1] The conversational style of speech is the only one that finds no place in church, though it is the training-ground for all public utterance. As Cowper said, " Pulpits for preaching; and the parlour, the garden, and the walk, for friendly and agreeable conversation." Quoted O. Elton, *A Survey of English Literature*, 1780–1830 (Arnold, 1920), " William Cowper," 1779, *Letters*. The lessons and prayers must not be made to sound like a series of casual remarks. Cp. Whately, *op. cit.*, Part IV, ch. iii, § 3.

[2] S.P.C.K.

has an interest supplied by the writer even more than by his material, and such books are valuable to us when we are often preaching, in that they keep up our interest in, and thought about, our work as we do it.

It would seem, however, as if we were likely to gain most from the study of kindred arts and sciences. We can learn much from the sister art of teaching and from the experience that has produced books on the theory of education. Books on psychology have much to tell us about interest and fatigue, about the formation of habits and the fundamental instincts of human nature.[1] Much guidance, and even direct " tips ", can be usefully gleaned from literary works on the nature of our mother tongue and what goes to make up style, and, for all Faust's gibe, his " famulus " Wagner was right when he quoted the saying that a priest could learn much from an actor. The same might be said of the barrister, the singer, the political " agitator ", and the man of letters.

But it is perhaps chiefly from the study of books on rhetoric that profit can be found, and here it seems that Whately was right when he said that " among the ancients, Aristotle, whose works are extant, may safely be pronounced to be also the best of systematic writers on rhetoric ".[2] Cicero's compositions, especially his *Brutus*, are full of good things. He speaks from his experience in the Roman law courts, but he does not really help us much. He was so sure that his Latin tongue could serve the purposes of eloquence and philosophy as well as could that of Athens, and was so delighted with his art, that he runs off into oratorical praises of oratory itself and, be it confessed, rather bores us. Quintilian, whose works are published with Aristotle's *Rhetoric* in the " Loeb Library ", throws much light on methods of education in the ancient world, but most later writers seem, after all, to derive from Aristotle either directly or through Cicero. Augustine in his *De Doctrina Christiana* lets us see something of how he used to teach at Milan and how he applied it to his preaching as a bishop. Whately is perhaps the most helpful of English lecturers on homiletics, but in his *Elements of Rhetoric* you feel he has been nurtured in the school of Aristotle. Newman tells us that it was Whately who opened his mind and taught him how to think, but, he added, " he had done his work towards me, or nearly so, when he had taught me to see with my own eyes and to walk

---

[1] I have worked this out more fully in a chapter, " The Psychology of Preaching, Evangelism and Edification ", in *Psychology and the Church*, ed. O. Hardman (Macmillan, 1925), pp. 163–185.

[2] *Op. cit.*, Introduction, § 2.

G

with my own feet ",[1] which is what the young preacher should learn
to do. That is the chief aim of all works of *Keryktik*,[2] as German
writers would have us call it, but which we prefer to think of as
homiletics or the art and science of sermon-writing.

v

To conclude. English seems likely to become the universal
world-language. In times past Greek, Latin, and French have in
turn made a bid for supremacy, and each has, one after the other,
seemed to have been on the verge of success. If we are to succeed
where they have failed, a great opportunity lies before us and a
great responsibility upon us. Our heritage of literature which
we have received to give in turn to the world is vast and varied, but
in what sort of English is it going to speak? If it is mere " pidgin "
English it will be a barbarous tongue. Mere " basic " English may
be a first step, but to stay there means a speech of the lowest grade.
If it is to be a dialect, it will be an immense loss. If it is to be spoken
through the nose or with a twang, then good-bye to poetry and
farewell to noble prose.

But it is not the mere vocabulary and its sounds that matter.
Our language has taken on a character from the past, and its words
are coloured with a thousand associations. Even if we do not " the
faith and morals hold that Milton held " (and I hope we don't share
either his Arianism or his views on divorce), as Wordsworth thought
we should, still

> " We must be free or die who speak the tongue
> That Shakespeare spake. . . ."

But beyond the resources and the richness of our vocabulary and
the simplicity and directness of our syntax, beyond the variety of
our poetry and the wealth of our prose, there is something indefin-
able, though directly felt, that is inextricably involved in our way of
speech. It has not been without consequence that as soon as the
English language was really formed it was Cranmer that taught our
mother tongue " to fold its hands and pray " in the words of the
Book of Common Prayer, that the phrases of the Authorised Version
of the Bible have been heard in church and have become household

---

[1] *Apologia*, Ch. I.
[2] G. W. Hervey, *A System of Christian Rhetoric for the Use of Preachers and
other Speakers* (London, 1873), Bk. IV, refers to Rudolf Stier's *Keryktik* in the
text, and in the index has references to Catachresis, Cataphasis, Cataplexis,
Cataploce or Parembole. The copies in the Bodleian at Oxford and in the
St. Deiniol's Library at Hawarden are uncut.

words which have entered into the finest fibres of our thought, that the Revised Version, without sacrificing sound, has furthered the beauty that lies in exact ideas embodied and interpreted in its sentences. This heritage, as well as our own spoken language, is what we are charged to convey to the whole world.

So we must not forget the part that may be played by the pulpit. The English used there will be heard by masses who seldom read, by men who have few books. The opportunity is shared by the broadcaster, but the sermon is, or may be, the more powerful instrument, because it speaks from the heart of the preacher to the heart of his hearers.

Still more in the Liturgy of the Church is there a power to sanctify speech, and, with speech, thought, since in the Liturgy the ideas conceived in the mind are taken into, and made to express, the inmost experience of the whole nature of man.

It is worth while taking trouble with the composition of your sermons and with their delivery by the voice.

APPENDIX I

HYMN SINGING. MELODIOUS INTELLIGENCE

" DON'T sing it like a hymn," our conductor said. " Please, remember that you are the Harmonic Choir." So I told him afterwards that, when men sang like that at our practices at King's College, I used to say. " This is a hymn that we're singing. Don't sing like the Harmonic Choir. Sing it as if it meant something."

I

People all round us are discussing the alleged decline in church attendance. They are saying that hymns are what people most care about. They are holding hymn-singing practices. Illustrated broadcast talks are being given by our leading musicians, and very good they are. Much excellent work is being done. But, with it all, things remain much the same. How does it come about that our conductor can still rate us like this?

Excellent as much of the work is, it is still mainly negative. We are told our faults, but we are not told how to cure them. We ourselves complain that the hymns are pitched too high for the congregation to sing or too low for the choirboys to get those beautiful head notes; that the organ drowns our voices, and that it does not give them enough support; that we cannot sing hymns that we do not know, and that we are tired of the old ones; that the music is drawled out, and that it is hurried and undignified. But do not all these " don'ts " miss the real defect—namely, lack of intelligence, and is not the real cure to think more about what we are singing?

II

What is it that too often makes the ordinary singing of hymns so deadly? Is it not that we sing them note by note, like Pomona when she read her romances aloud in *Rudder Grange*—" The La-dy-ce-cil-ia-seiz-ed-the-dag-ger-and-held-it-a-loft-drip-ping-with-jore." That is the way a child reads in an infant school, but not the way an ordinary church-goer reads a book. As we read our eyes and our attention are already at the end of the sentence that we are reading. In reading aloud we mentally keep half a line ahead of the words we utter. So we phrase each sentence as a whole and vary the rhythm with alternating stress.

In all intelligent singing we think the sounds ahead of those we are singing. Our eyes are on the notes three or four in front. We sing by bars and phrases. Automatically we stress some notes, and, while keeping the rhythm steady, slightly vary the force and length of the others. Sir Walford Davies used to tell us that Chopin was reported to have said: " I keep strict time with my left hand and let my right do what it likes."

So each syllable of a hymn must be sung, not as a thing by itself, but as part of a line, and each line as a part of a verse. A verse has a unity of its own which should not be broken. If this is once realised we shall get rid, not indeed of that pause at the end of a line, which may be intended, written in the music and demanded by the rhythm of the line, but of that gasp for breath and hesitation at the beginning of the next which marks a restarting of thought, delaying the action of speech and melody. In the old days of horse traction it was said that it was the continual effort of starting the trams that wore out the horses.

III

But the verse is itself a unit of a larger whole, not a thing by itself. The whole hymn is, or should be, a lyric unity, and a lyric is generally of three or, as in the case of a ballad of, at most, four verses. A Welshman is a lyric poet by nature, and Welsh hymns have their limitations, but Welsh hymnody is an art, and a living art. A glance at a Welsh hymnal will show that not only has each verse, as a rule, its complex and varied structure, but also that each hymn is rarely of more than three verses.

If we can realise the unity of a hymn we shall be very sparing in our use of the little four-line, ballad-like, hymns, with their small scope for melody or verbal construction. Instinctively we shall prefer for praise the strong choral tunes and finely balanced stanzas with fewer verses but richer construction. We shall automatically pause for one silent bar at the end of each verse, sustaining our attention, through the rest, on to the next, and so avoid that aggravating dawdling *rallentando* at the end of each final line, sung as if we were exhausted by the effort of singing four or even eight others, and we shall reserve the slowing of pace for the dignity of the doxology or the consummation of the poem.

The use of intelligence is what really matters. If we can get this sense of virile reality into our hymn-singing, the other reforms will easily come of themselves. If we sing in unison, we shall realise the necessity of transposing our melodies down to a pitch considerably lower and nearer to that of our natural speaking voices. It will no longer be necessary for the organist to pull out all the stops to drag us on by sheer mechanised force, but we shall probably demand a choir-ruler or conductor. He will not " play over " the first line softly with a *rallentando* at the end which starts people off dragging the music, so that he has to drown their voices to get them along; but he will give a clear intonation, even a little quicker than he wishes the whole hymn to be sung, so that the congregation, instead of shuffling their feet in rising half-way through the first line, will stand up at once and he will be able to accompany them lightly and softly.

IV

People will probably want to have practices, and would soon learn to sing in parts, as the Welsh do. Better hymns would become popular and be asked for. Slow singing would come from restraint of energy, and not be a mere sign of slackness. Soft singing would be the normal custom, but it would gather volume by being soft singing by many voices, and loud singing as the exception would sound far louder in praise. Moreover, the organist, restraining himself to accompany, would be listened to when, in his " voluntaries ", which he often plays so well at the beginning and end of the services, he has his opportunity to show his skill in interpreting the work of some great master.

(Reprinted by permission from the *Church Times*, November 28, 1941.)

APPENDIX II

PREACHING AND STYLE. THE STRUCTURE OF CLEAR SPEAKING

" Le Style est (de) l'homme même."

—*Oeuvres complètes de Buffon* (Paris, Garnier), Tome douzième, p. 330. Discours prononcé a l'Academie Française par M. de Buffon le jour de sa reception, 1753.

THERE is a well-known quotation which is often misapplied and still more often misquoted. *Le Style est l'homme même* does not mean that style is the man in the sense that command of words, like manners, " makyth man ", but that it is what a man is that gives him the power in speech.

So writers of books on preaching are fond of emphasising the value of the personal note in sermons. They are fond of quoting the sound, but rather obvious and not very helpful, information given by the old clergyman to the inquiring student of pastoral theology: " Some men prepare their sermons (impressive pause), *others prepare themselves.*" It is not enough merely to be good in order to be a good preacher. There is a value in the possession of style. It enables a man to write books, as Boswell aimed at and succeeded in doing, that men want to read. It gives a preacher power to make men listen to him and understand what he says. How is it to be acquired?

I

Men in France had been interested in the problem for over two centuries before Buffon wrote. He came at the end of a long series of others who had thought on the matter. Du Bellay had pleaded, as had Dante in Italy before him, for the use of the vernacular. The French language, in which men thought, had to be set free from the influence of its mother Latin and purged of Gongorism or imitation of Spanish. The exact use of words had to be settled. The pedantry of Euphuism, which found delight in mere manipulation of speech, had to be simplified. The love of sound had to be put in its place as a secondary matter compared with the conveying of meaning. Preachers tended to over-emphasise rhetoric. Salons

of learned ladies were tempted to make conversation " precious ".
The use of the silent pen evolved the art of letter-writing.

Men strove for simplicity. The language used should be that of
the plain man. Its first quality must be that of pleasing, or no one
will listen to you. But the art of reasoning and logic must have its
place, and clarity wins conviction. The French language, Voltaire
said, was fixed by Pascal's writing in the form of *Letters to a Provincial*
in language based on everyday speech. He prepared to write a
book, for which he jotted down his *Thoughts* just as they came to him
fresh from the mint of his brain. For it takes time to cover the
ground, and completeness, proportion, and balance of thought in
selecting and arranging material are essential to good writing. But
you can't criticise, select and arrange material unless you know
how to think, so Antoine Arnauld wrote his beautifully clear *Logic
of Port Royal*. Bossuet preached from the pulpit sermons which have
the rare merit of being literature as well as homilies. The establishment of the French Academy settled the meaning of words without
which there can be no exact expression of ideas, and so established
French prose on the throne to the cost of poetry for many a long year.

II

Buffon came at the end of this long history of interest in language
and style, and he summed up the result in his *Discourse Pronounced at
the French Academy on the Day of his Reception as a Member* in 1753.

After the usual compliments he begins by pointing out how " in
all days men have known how to rule and lead (commander) others
by the power of words ", but that " good speech and good writing
are only found in enlightened ages ". They are the outcome of
general civilisation, the accompaniment of a long process in education. " True eloquence presupposes the exercise of genius and
culture of the mind ", which is something very different from the
mere talent of natural speech, a thing which all men with strong
passions, supple tongues and lips (*organes*), and quick imaginations,
possess. To sway a crowd you only want a strong and pathetic
voice, frequent expressive glances, and a flood of fine-sounding
words. But this is rhetoric, not style, and appeals only to the
groundlings. For the minority who have steady heads,

> " you must have facts, thoughts, and reasons. You must know
> how to present them, to give them shades of meaning [*les
> nuancer*], to set them in order. It is not enough to strike the
> ear and to catch [*occuper*] the eye. You must influence the
> soul and touch the heart as you speak to the mind."

Style lies in the balance and sequence of ideas rather than in the harmony of sound :—

" If you connect them straitly, if you link them together, it becomes firm, nervous, and concise. If you let them just follow one another [*se succéder lentement*], and only connect them by the help of words, however choice [*elégants*] they may be, the style will be diffuse, slack and trailing."

So, he says, the first thing is to make a plan of the chief leading ideas. Going back to this again and again will determine the right spacing of subsidiary and explanatory ideas, and will put general and particular ideas in true perspective. It will weed out barren ideas and, by the working of your mind, will gradually bring a unity into the whole. This is the only way to strengthen and raise your thoughts. The more work you put into your thinking (*méditation*) the easier it will be to express them.

This is not style yet, but it is its foundation. Without it the writer will lose his way (*s'égare*), let his pen run on, and bring in irrelevances. The construction will be bad, and readers, while admiring the author's cleverness (*esprit*), will see that he lacks genius. For this very reason people who talk quite well and write as they speak write quite badly. There are so many works made up of shreds and patches (*pièces de rapport*) and so few moulded in a single casting (*qui sont fondu d'un seul jet*). For—

" Every subject has a unity in itself and can be treated as a single theme. Without this the details become interruptions and the whole becomes confused and tedious instead of being a coherent and solid work."

It is this lack of plan, due to not having thought enough before beginning to write, that bothers a clever man. He doesn't know how to begin. His ideas are unbalanced. They tumble over one another. But directly he makes his outline and has put down the essentials in order—

" he enjoys writing. Ideas come naturally to birth. Words flow freely. His style becomes natural and easy. He warms to his subject. His matter takes on colour. Feeling and insight grow and carry him on. What he has said leads him on to what he goes on to say and his style becomes interesting, luminous, and brilliant."

So to write well you must know your subject. You must be able to see clearly the order of your thoughts, to string them together so

that when you start writing you keep them to scale. Only this can
make what you write simple, clear, alive, direct, and of a piece
(*suivant*).

If you keep to terms of common speech, your writing will be
noble. If you distrust all that is merely brilliant, equivocal, and
witty, it will be weighty, even majestic, and, finally, if you write as
you think, if you are yourself convinced, your good faith with
yourself will have its effect—if only you don't overdo it, if you write
with more honesty than confidence, with more reason than heat.

Then he sums up and recapitulates what he has said to lead up
to his climax:—

> "To write well you must, all at once, think well, feel well,
> and express yourself well. You must have, at the same time,
> wits, and soul, and taste. Style presupposes the combined
> exercise of all the powers of the mind. Ideas alone form the
> foundation of style. The harmony of words is but an accessory
> which comes by practice."

Then comes the immediate context of the famous quotation :—

> "Well-written works are the only works that live for poster-
> ity. Knowledge, wealth, numbers, masses, originality [*par-
> ticularités*] or novelty of facts give no guarantees of immortality.
> Works that deal with small matters, without taste, nobility or
> genius, pass away or are better treated by others more clever.
> All these things are from outside the man. *Style is (comes from)
> the man himself* [*Le Style est (de) l'homme même*].
>
> "Style, therefore, cannot be elevated, or tacked on [*se
> transporter*], nor be fashioned [*s'altérer*]. If it is high, noble,
> sublime, its author will be no less admired for all time. For only
> truth endures and never dies."

Again, he goes on, a good style is only really good by the endless
number of truths that it presents. All the beauties of the mind found
in it, all the links (*rapports*) of which it is composed, are so many
truths as useful, and maybe more precious, for the mind of man than
those which may form the ground on which the subject treated of is
based. And so he passes on to his peroration to drive his conclusion
home.

III

How does all this apply to sermons? What is the lesson taught
by pastoral theology? What, first of all, are the preliminary stages
necessary if personality is to tell in the pulpit?

First, *know your subject well*. Take plenty of time to gather and collect your thoughts. Don't fancy that it will do to begin thinking about your Sunday sermon the Monday before when you meet " to settle the work for the week ". It takes more than a week to make a sermon. But, on the other hand, you can have several building up on the stocks at the same time.

Secondly, style lies primarily in the order, balance and movement of your thought. Therefore, *first make an outline of what you want to say*. See it first before you hear it. Get a pattern into it. It should have a " beginning, a middle, and an end ", as Aristotle said a play should have. Sort it so that one part leads on without any jolt to the next.

Then, finally, *write it out, hearing what you are saying as you write*. You will find no difficulty in this after a little practice. As you write resist any temptation to introduce new ideas not in the original plan. That may do in a conversation, but not in a sermon, where your time is limited.

Use the words of everyday life. Let them be concrete rather than abstract. If the subject prompts it, you will write with direct-ness and feeling, but don't try to add purple patches or rhetorical phrases that don't come naturally. Illustrations should have been thought out before. As you write imagine yourself actually speaking in the pulpit, with your congregation before you. Learn to write as you speak, and to speak as you write. If you have the right ideas they will come out all right. For, in writing, as Buffon said, *Style comes from the man himself.*

(Reprinted, by permission, from the *Church Times*, April 1, 1943.)

APPENDIX III

SUBJECTS FOR SERMONS FOR THREE MONTHS AHEAD

Dates	Subjects for Sermons
Oct. 4.	
Harvest Festival	Thankfulness. (A.)
19th Sunday after	Natural Science and Religion. (B.)
Trinity.	The Theistic Argument from Design.
	The Sermon on the Mount:
	The old and the new law, The letter and the spirit, Negative and positive morality.
Oct. 11.	
20th Sunday after	The Poor in Spirit and Riches.
Trinity.	The Apostles Creed and its Origin from Baptism Preparation.
Oct. 18.	How St. Luke Wrote his Gospel. (B.)
St. Luke's Day	Is Avoidance of Pain the Only Thing that
21st Sunday after	Matters?
Trinity.	Hedonism and Christianity.
	Why Christian Science is Unchristian.
	They that Mourn. The Problem of Pain.
Oct. 25.	The Nicene Creed. The Issue at the Council
22nd Sunday after	of Nicaea.
Trinity.	The Inheritance of the Meek—Readiness to Learn.
Nov. 1.	What is a Saint? (A.)
All Saints Day	Unknown Saints, *e.g.*, Epaphras.
23rd Sunday after	The Accusation that the Church of England
Trinity.	Produces no Saints.
	The Gentleman and the Saint.
	Prayer for the Dead.
Nov. 8.	The Blessing on the Merciful.
24th Sunday after	The Purpose of Punishment.
Trinity.	Revenge and Forgiveness—Which is the Strong Position?

94

Nov. 8 (*cont.*)   Why Astrology is Wrong.
What We can Learn from Hymns (illustrated by three examples).

Nov. 15.
25th Sunday after Trinity.

The Blessing of the Pure in Heart.
Single-mindedness and Doing Your Particular Duty.
God-parents.
  How they arose.
  Practical suggestions as to what they might do.

Nov. 22.
Last Sunday after Trinity.

The Feeding of the Five Thousand (the Gosepl for the Day). (A.)
The Holy Communion (on Christmas Day). (A.)
Why is it Wrong to Waste? (B.)
The Value of Little Things (" Two Small Fishes "). (B.)
The Harm of Religious Bribery. (B.)
The Value of Organisation.
  In the practical work of the Church. (B.)
  In teaching and the Calendar.

Nov. 29.
Advent I.

The Coming of Christ. (A.)
Has the Second Coming already Taken Place at Pentecost?
Death. (A.)
Why We Believe in Immortality. (B.)
Practical Differences the Belief in the Future Life Makes.
The Resurrection of the Body.

Dec. 6.
Advent II.
" Bible Sunday "

Judgment. (A.)
The Nature of Judgment.
Impossibility of Judging Others Fairly.
Judgment of Sin and of the Sinner.
" The Bible." (A.)
What is Inspiration?
How were the Gospels Written?
How were the Books of the New Testament Chosen?
The Limitations and Value of the Old Testament.

Dec. 13.   Heaven. (A.)
    Advent III.   Is Heaven a Place or a State?   (B.)
                    What do We Mean by the Right Hand of
                        God?
                    The Use of Symbolical Language.

Dec. 20.   Hell. (A.)
    Advent IV.   Is Fear a Right Motive for Doing Right?
    " Ordination   Has the Threat of Hell ever Succeeded?
    Sunday "   What is the Purpose of Punishment?
                    Holy Orders. (A.)
                    Episcopacy.
                        Its history in the early Church.
                    The doctrine of Apostolic Succession.

The above table is based on the results of two classes or lectures
in homiletics repeated, with some variations, over a period of some
fifteen years.   The first was on the making out a scehme for three
months ahead, and the second, in which the Introduction of Phillips
Brooks' Sermon "Make the Men Sit Down," was analysed and then
suggestions were asked for other subjects which the Feeding of the
Five Thousand might be used to introduce.

Practically the same suggestions were made every year.   These
are marked (A).   It will be seen that they are obvious, very general,
wide and indefinite.   Those marked (B) are some of the more
definite and less vague, elicited by questions, and often by rather
leading questions.   Those on the Feeding of the Five Thousand
were generally all elicited from the class in the last half-hour of the
lecture.   The other are various subjects suggested by the lecturer
at the end of the lecture, at various other times, or put up on the
notice-board by way of further suggestions.

The student should make out similar tables for himself for the
other three quarters of the year.

APPENDIX IV
A THREE MONTHS' PLAN FOR SERMONS THREE TIMES A WEEK

	SUNDAY MORNING. Doctrinal Subjects: The Creed.	SUNDAY EVENING. Moral Subjects: The Ten Commandments.	WEDNESDAY EVENING. Devotional Subjects: The Prayer Book.
April 22. Low Sunday.	*The Evidence for the Resurrection.* (a) The Witnesses Ample. (b) Telling Different Things. (c) With Nothing to Gain.	*The Resurrection: Proving the Claim of Christ.* (a) His Claim in Acts. (b) His Claim in Words. (c) The Attempts to Disprove it Countered.	*The Resurrection and Our Hope of Immortality.* (a) Christ's Endorsing Jewish Belief. (b) All Life from God. (c) The Fact of His Resurrection.
April 29.	*One God.* (a) Unity in Material Nature. (b) Unity in Living Nature. (c) Unity in Spiritual Nature (or Nature Worship; Polytheism amd Monotheism) (or The Four Arguments for Theism).	*The First Commandment: Practical Result of Belief in One God—" One God, One Law."* (a) In all Places. (b) For all Classes. (c) For Both Sexes.	*The Practice of the Presence of God.* (a) Daily Private Prayer. (b) Weekly Common Prayer. (c) On Special Occasions.
May 6.	*The Incarnation: Christ as very God.* (a) Arianism and the Nicene Creed. (b) Why it Mattered. (c) Only Christians know God.	*The Second Commandment and Sacramentalism.* (a) The Danger of Idolatry. (b) God can be pictured on Christ. (c) Symbolism inadequate but necessary.	*Baptism—Spiritual Growth and Habit.* (a) New Birth and Growth. (b) Rival Theory of Conversion. (c) Growth and Habit in the Church.
May 13.	*The Human Life of Christ: " Very Man."* (a) Apollinarianism and Nestorianism. (b) Value and Defects of Unitarianism. (c) Only Christians understand Human Nature.	*The Third Commandment and Sincerity in Speech.* (a) Only Man has Speech. (b) Responsibility for Right Use. (c) Depends on Sense of the Presence of God.	*Prayer—Private and Common.* (a) Their Relative Importance. (b) History of Daily Service. (c) Books of Private Prayer.
May 20.	*The Atonement: Wrong and True Theories —A Fact of Experience.* (a) Propitiation of an Angry God. (b) Ransom — by a Payment to the Devil. (c) Substitution of Innocent for the Guilty. (d) Union with Christ and His Cross.	*The Fourth Commandment: Care of our Time.* (a) The Duty of Work. (b) The Value of Rest. (c) The Keeping of Sunday.	*The Eucharist as a Sacrifice.* (a) Christ's Command. (b) History of Christian Worship. (c) Worship and " getting Good."

	SUNDAY MORNING. Doctrinal Subjects: The Creed.	SUNDAY EVENING. Moral Subjects: The Ten Commandments.	WEDNESDAY EVENING. Devotional Subjects: The Prayer Book.
May 24. Thursday. Ascension Day.	*The Ascension and Modern Science.* (a) Old Idea of Heaven. (b) Modern Astronomy. (c) God Present Everywhere.	*Duty and Aims, I.* (a) In Material Things. (b) In Intellectual Things. (c) In Spiritual Things.	*Communion, I.* (a) Ideas of Mystics. (b) Ideas of Sacramentalists. (c) The Prayer of Humble Access.
May 27.	*The Things that are Above.* (a) Retention of Old Language. (b) The Meaning of "Above." (c) The "Right Hand of God" wherever He Works.	*Duty and Aims, II.* (a) Towards God. (b) Towards Our Neighbour. (c) To Ourselves.	*Communion, II.* (a) "He in us"—individualistic. (b) "We in Him"—corporate. (c) Also in Confirmation, and in the Daily Office.
June 3. Whitsun Day.	*The Holy Spirit and Inspiration.* (a) The Guidance of the Church. (b) Inspiration of the Bible. (c) The Voice of Conscience.	*The Letter and the Spirit in the Ten Commandments and the Sermon on the Mount.* (a) Acts and Motives. (b) Negative and Positive. (c) The Conflict of Duties.	*The Bible and Devotional Reading.* (a) Following the Daily Service. (b) Reading for Study. (c) Meditation.
June 10. Trinity Sunday.	*The Doctrine of the Trinity.* (a) Arising from Attacks of Jews and Greeks. (b) Discussions by Theologians and Council. (c) The Old Problem of the One and the Many.	*The Unity and Variety of the World.* (a) On the Material Order of Stones, Plants, Animals, and Man. (b) Unity or Uniformity. (c) Supremely in God.	*The Christian Year.* (a) Taking Things in Order. (b) Fast and Festival. (c) The Calendar.
June 17. 1st Sunday after Trinity.	*The Church.* (a) Apostolic Succession. (b) Individual and Corporate Christianity. (c) Authority of the Combined Experience of Others.	*The Fifth Commandment: Honouring All Men.* (a) Respect for Superiors. (b) Respect for Inferiors. (c) "That State of Life," etc.	*Intercession.* (a) In Private Prayer. (b) The Litany in Public Prayer and the Eucharist. (c) The Use of Books.
June 23. 2nd Sunday after Trinity.	*Sacramentalism.* (a) Man, Body and Soul. (b) Christ—God and Man. (c) Outward Visible Signs and Inward Spiritual Grace.	*The Sixth Commandment: The Instinct of Anger.* (a) Its Psychology. (b) Respect for Human Life. (c) Private Revenge and State Justice.	*Self Examination.* (a) Danger of Introspection. (b) Value in Facing Moral Issues. (c) "Being Sorry, Owning Up, and doing your Best to Make Up."

APPENDIX V

SUBJECTS ASKED FOR AT A PADRE'S HOUR

THE following " Examples of Subjects selected by Soldiers for Padre's Hours " is reprinted by permission from *Notes for Service Chaplains*. No. 1, " Experiments in Religious Education " (London: The Churches' Committee for Supplementing Religious Education among Men in H.M. Forces (C.C.M.F.), Townsend House, Greycoat Place, S.W.). Price 6*d*.

A. *Religion*

1. Is religion primitive superstition and fear?
2. Is religion wishful-thinking make-believe?
3. Is religion " the opium of the masses " ?
4. Can a man live without religion?
5. How can we know ours is the true religion? Do not all religions claim to be true?
6. What right have we to change other people's religions? Is not one religion as good or bad as another? Have not people got the religion most suitable to them?

B. *God*

7. How can we know there is a God?
8. Which of the many is the true God?
9. Has not modern knowledge destroyed the old belief in God?

C. *Jesus Christ*

10. Was Jesus " God on earth " ?
11. Was Jesus just an outstanding religious man?
12. Did Jesus rise from the dead?
13. Are the accounts of His miracles true?
14. Was not Jesus a Pacifist?

D. *The Church*

15. Why are there so many Churches? Which is the true one?
16. What good has the Church done in the world?
17. Are not the Churches dying out?
18. Why do Nazis and Communists persecute the Churches?

H

E. Bible

19. Is the Bible the infallible Word of God?
20. Is the Bible out of date?
21. The Bibles of other religions?

F. Worship and Means of Grace

22. What is the good of worship?
23. Is prayer of any use?
24. Why should soldiers be compelled to go to church?
25. Can a man live the Christian life without going to church?

G. Immortality

26. Do we rise from the dead?   How?
27. Is Spiritualism true?
28. Is there a heaven and hell?
29. When is the end of the world?

H. Other Religions

30. What is the religion of Japan?
31. What are the religions of India?
32. What is the religion of China?
33. Why are the Jews hated and persecuted?

I. War

34. Why does God allow war and innocent suffering?
35. Can a Christian be a soldier?
36. How can you reconcile war and the Gospel of Love?
37. Should we not give up religion during war?
38. Does God " take sides " in war, or is He non-belligerent?

J. Ethical Problems

39. Is freedom of the will real?
40. Do you believe in fate and astrology?
41. How can human nature be changed?
42. " There will always be a war "?
43. How can we prevent future wars?
44. Why did the Churches not stop this war?
45. Why are the Churches reactionary?
46. Should the Church interfere in politics and social affairs?
47. Why does the Church allow race and colour bars?

48. What is wrong in fornication (if both the man and woman want it)?
49. Why does the Church condemn birth control?
50. Why does the Church condemn divorce?
51. What are the Churches doing for post-war reconstruction?
52. Will the world ever be perfect?

APPENDIX VI

THE LEGITIMATE USE OF THE SERMONS OF OTHERS

Phillips Brooks begins a sermon on the Feeding of the Five Thousand (*Twenty Sermons*, Macmillan, 1899, Sermon XIII, "Make the Men Sit Down," p. 226), thus : " And Jesus said, Make the men sit down."—John vi, 10.

It was on the farther side of the Sea of Tiberias, a region which Christ seldom visited, a region which is to-day a wilderness. A multitude had followed the Lord across the water and were filling the empty place with crowd, and clamour, and confusion. Curiosity was all alive. What He had done last, what He would do next, was flying about in question and answer from mouth to mouth. The scene was full of movement. Every man was on his feet. Old friends were meeting. Christ's were eagerly pleading for him. The enemies of Christ were violently claiming that He was an impostor. Gestures were furious; words came fast; faces glowed; eyes sparkled; feet hurried back and forth. Such is the picture which seems to paint itself before us in the first verses of this sixth chapter of St. John.

And then there comes a change. The midday sun grows hot. Hunger and exhaustion take possession of these excited frames. The need of rest overcomes the eagerness of action. And out of the midst of the flagging tumult comes the calm voice of Jesus, saying to the disciples who are closest to him, " Make the men sit down." And the disciples pass here and there through the crowd, doing their Master's will, until five thousand men are seated on the grass.

Then a new scene appears. Quiet has come in the place of noise; repose instead of action. Faces which just now were flushed and excited have grown calm. And, what is really at the heart of all, there is a change in the whole crowd's activity. It has become receptive. It is waiting to be fed. Not only with the barley loaves and fishes. The presence of Christ is before it, and it receives that. By and by the words of Christ fall on it and it receives them, until at last there begins to break forth from the seated ranks the declaration that they have indeed received Him, and they whisper to one another, " This is indeed the prophet that should come into the world."

This is the meaning which I find in the words of Jesus when He said to His disciples, " Make the men sit down." It is the change from the active and restless to the receptive and quiet state, from the condition in which all the life was flowing outward in eager self-assertion to the other condition in which the life was being influenced, that is being flowed upon by the richer power which came forth from Him.

I

This introduction may be analysed, and visualised, thus :—

(a) The crowd that followed our Lord.
  Noise and confusion.
    Advocates and opponents.

(b) A change as the sun grows hot.
  Eager men getting tired.
    Christ says, " Make the men sit down."

(c) An inner change is each
  Becoming receptive—waiting to be fed.
    Realising whom they have received.

(d) The lesson of the story.
  Self-assertion *v.* receptiveness.

II

It may be recast, when assimilated and coming up again as an introduction to the ideas of " The Need of Organisation ", thus :—

(a) A crowd always an interesting sight.
  Especially when united by a common aim.
    Combining its forces into one.

(b) Such a crowd following our Lord.
  Made up of all sorts—an epitome of the nation.
    Excited—acting and reacting—away from normal influences.

(c) A change as they grow tired.
  A voice, " Make the men sit down."
    Necessary if to be fed—a whole, not a mob.

(d) The passage chosen twice for the Gospel. In Lent.
  The last Sunday after Trinity—the value of organisation.
    Looking forward to a new Church Year.

III

The following opening was written and preached from such an outline :—

A crowd is always an interesting sight. Where many men are gathered together we mark their differences in bearing and the variety of their features. The mere succession of contrasted faces attracts our notice, and if we begin to let our speculations run on, the interest increases. The natural curiosity that we all feel about individuals is multiplied by the numbers that pass before us. We get a vague but stirring sense of the size of the world.

Especially is this true of a crowd of men united by a common aim. The lined-up ranks of citizens waiting for royalty to pass, the sea of up-turned faces when men are hanging on the words of a speaker, the onward sweep of a stream of people flowing out to see some great sight—a football match or some great review—all have an additional interest for us. For when bent all on one purpose the forces of individuals, so varied and different in themselves, are fused into one. The problem of meeting such a common demand is always one of intensest interest.

Such a crowd was following our Lord. It was made up of all sorts. Men and women, rich and poor, young and old, simple and learned, all were there. It was an epitome of the nation. It was a type of the world. Drawn together, though so different, by the common attraction of Christ's teaching, they were excited, nervous, exalted above themselves. Their excitement acted and reacted in each on one another. They had left their homes and villages; they were away from all the normal and steadying influences involved in the life they usually lived. Men were arguing. Women were gathering together. Children were running about. All was confused, alert, strained, alive.

Then came a change. It is impossible to keep up mere excitement. The sun grew hot. The people had come far. They were physically tired. They felt hungry. They were becoming exhausted. Reaction was setting in, when through the lessening confusion a voice was heard, " Make the men sit down." It was spoken to the disciples, who quickly, quietly, and decidedly, as men who knew their work, grouped the people by companies, made them sit down on the grass and wait. It was necessary to get order if they were to be fed. The fluid mass of men became an organic whole, and was no longer a mob.

So in our Prayer Book this passage is chosen twice for the Sunday

Gospel. Once in the middle of Lent—on Refreshment Sunday, when it is the idea of the feeding of the people that is prominent in our minds and we naturally think of the spiritual food of the Body and Blood of Christ that we are preparing to receive in our Easter Communion—and once before Advent, on the last Sunday after Trinity, just before the beginning of the new Church Year. Then it is the idea of the value of organisation that comes forward in our minds—the need of order and co-operation if men are to be fed.

APPENDIX VII

ABSTRACT AND CONCRETE OR GENERALS AND PARTICULARS

"To me it seems that, if we begin with things particular and concrete, and thence proceed to general notions and conclusions, there will be no difficulty in this matter. But if we begin with generalities, and lay our foundation in abstract ideas, we shall find ourselves entangled and lost in a labyrinth of our own making."—Bp. Berkeley, *Alciphron*, "The Seventh Dialogue," 20.

WHAT makes sermons so dull? Why do they leave so little impression behind? Why must we acknowledge that if the members of any ordinary congregation were stopped at the church door and were asked why they believed in God, nine out of ten would be unable to give a clear answer? "Our religion is in a book," said Dr. Johnson. "We have an order of men whose duty it is to teach it; we have one day in the week set apart for it, and this is in general pretty well observed; yet ask the ten first gross men you meet and hear what they can tell of their religion." [1]

We have a wonderful opportunity in our thousands of pulpits, but it is missed. Sermons are proverbially tedious—to "sermonise" is to be a bore. Feeble jokes about their soporific effect are heard everywhere. George Eliot could talk of "that bright and cheerful air which a sermon is often observed to produce when it is quite finished".[2] "*Ich kann das Predigt nicht vertragen*" ("I can't stand sermons"), said Goethe.[3] What justifies these complaints? For in every age men have complained that they are not practical enough, that they are not sufficiently simple, that they are too simple, that they are platitudinous, that there is nothing in them, that preachers try to get too much into them, that they use words men do not understand. "There is great need", says the *Final Report of the Archbishops' Commission on Training for the Ministry*, "that full attention should be given to training Ordinands in the power of translating the technical language of Theology in terms understood by ordinary people." [4]

[1] Boswell's *Life*, Fri. 26–Mon. 29 April, 1776 (ed. G. B. Hull and L. F. Powell, Oxford, 1834), Vol. III, p. 50.
[2] *Scenes from Clerical Life*, "Mr. Gilfil's Love Story," Ch. XI.
[3] *Sprüche in Prosa*, Sechste Abtheilung.
[4] *Training for the Ministry* (Press and Publications Board of the Church Assembly), 1944, § 107.

I

What is the matter with sermons to-day? The reasons for these complaints are many, but perhaps one is the chief. Sermons are full of abstract ideas when they should give concrete facts. They are couched in general terms when they should give particular instances. They are full of words of Norman–French origin when they should use the plain, honest, Saxon terms of our daily speech.

This, of course, is no new thing, and does not apply only to sermons. In philosophy more than two thousand years ago Aristotle said, " In reasoning about matters of conduct general statements are too vague, and do not contain so much truth as particular propositions, for conduct is concerned with particulars." [1] In literature, we find Boswell's story of the *Life of Dr. Johnson* " full of quotations ", while the Johnsonese of the Doctor himself in his *Rasselas* frankly bores us and, as did Mary Smith when at Cranford, Miss Matty insisted on reading all Miss Deborah Jekyns' letters right through, we long for " facts instead of reflections ".[2] In the drama, Lord Kames, in his *Elements of Criticism of Shakespere* (1762), showed " that the merit of his language lay in the absence of those general terms which was the blemish of the [eighteenth] century's own diction ", saying that " Shakespere's style in that respect is excellent: every article in his descriptions is particular as in nature." [3] So, too, in art we are impatient of Watts' personifications of time, death, and judgment, of hope and all the rest, for all that we admire his portraits and his Man that had Great Possessions. We are inclined to side, not with Sir Joshua Reynolds, who held that " the Grand Style in Painting consists in an abstract and general treatment of objects and not fidelity to particulars ",[4] but with " gentle, visionary

---

[1] *Eth. Nic.*, Bk. II, Ch. vii, § 1, 1107a. Cp. Bk. VI, Ch. iv, § 4, 1143b. " General rules are based on particular cases."

[2] *Cranford*, Ch. V, " Old Letters."

[3] Quoted in *Eighteenth-Century Essays*, ed. D. Nichol Smith (Glasgow, Maclehose, 1903), p. xxxiv.

[4] O. Elton, *Survey of English Literature*, 1830–1880, Vol. I, p. 221: " Reynolds he [Ruskin] was to attack, ten years later, respectfully and strongly, for his heresy " (already well denounced by Blake) that " the grand style in painting consists in an abstract and general treatment of the objects, and not in fidelity to particulars ".

See *The Discourses of Sir Joshua Reynolds* (World's Classics, cxlix, Oxford, 1907), Discourses III and IV *passim*. *E.g.*, p. 26: " The whole beauty and grandeur of the art (of painting) consists, in my opinion, in being able to get above all singular forms, local customs, particularities, and details of every kind." P. 36: " Perfect form is produced by leaving out particularities,

Blake ", who said that " he who would do good to another, must do
it in minute particulars ", even if we do not go so far as to say with
him that " to generalise is to be an idiot ".[1]

So, in homiletics, Hooker, after quoting the words of Aristotle
cited above, adds, with reference to the preachers of his day and their
congregations :—

> " With gross and popular capacities nothing doth more
> prevail than unlimited generalities because of their plainness at
> first sight; nothing less with men of exact judgement, because
> such rules are not safe to be trusted over far." [2]

And Jeremy Taylor, realising, like George Herbert, that for
country people " Scholars ought to be diligent . . . in driving of
their general Schoole rules ever to the smallest actions of life ",[3]
when giving his *Rules and Advice to the Clergy of Down and Connor for
their deportment in their personal and public Capacities* said, in giving
" Rules and advice concerning preaching " :—

> " Do not spend your sermons on general and indefinite
> things, as in exhortations to people to get Christ, to be united to
> Christ; and things of the like unlimited signification; but tell
> them in every duty what are the measures, what circumstances,
> what instruments, and what is the particular minute meaning

---

and retaining only general ideas," and the final words of the Fourth Discourse, " There is but one presiding principle which regulates and gives
stability to every art. The works, whether of poets, painters, moralists, or
historians, which are built upon general nature, live for ever; while those
which depend for their existence on particular customs and habits, a partial
view of nature, or the fluctuations of fashion, can only be coeval with that
which first raised them from obscurity. Present time and future may be
considered as rivals; and he who solicits the one must expect to be dis-
countenanced by the other."

[1] Quoted in A. Gilchrist's *Life of William Blake* (Macmillan, 1880),
Vol. I, p. 235. Blake continues:
" General good is the plea of the scoundrel, hypocrite, and flatterer.
For Art and Science cannot exist but in minutely organised particulars,
And not in generalizing demonstrations of the Rational Power.
The Infinite alone resides in definite and determinate identity."

[2] *Ecclesiastical Polity*, Bk. V, Ch. ix, § 2. The words immediately
preceding are: " General rules, till their limits be fully known (especially
in matters of public and ecclesiastical affairs), are by reason of their manifold
exceptions which lie hidden in them, no other to the eye of man's understanding than cloudy mists cast before the eye of common sense."

[3] *A Priest to the Temple, or The Countrey Parson*, Ch. XXVI, " The Parson's
Eve."

of every general advice. For generals not explicated do but fill people's heads with empty notions, and their mouths with perpetual unintelligible talk; but their hearts remain empty, and themselves are not edified." [1]

II

Let us try to get to the root of the matter. There is a great value in generalising. " Some have said ", declared Dr. Inge out-spokenly, " that human beings are not moved by abstractions; the truth is that they are seldom moved by anything else." [2] Aristotle, while asserting that " thought by itself moves nothing ", recognised that " true theories are exceedingly useful, not only as a means of knowledge, but also as guides of life ".[3] The difficult lessons so wonderfully learned even by infants when they realise how many beans make five and get the conception of abstract numbers are the necessary foundation for all commerce and civilisation. For general terms are counters used for summing up, and dealing with, complex ideas, as when in mathematics you represent a complicated unity by a letter " x ". Technical terms sum up elaborate combinations of data and save us from the necessity of repeated descriptions. " An algebraical formula ", writes M. Henri Poincaré, " which gives us the solution of a type of numerical problems if we finally replace the letters by numbers . . . saves us the trouble of a constant repetition of numerical calculation." [4] The wiseacres of Laputa who tried to get rid of words by carrying about with them specimens of the things they represented, since, as they said, " words are only names for things ", laid a burden upon their back too heavy to be borne, and made conversation a most difficult art.[5] We can't do without abstract nouns and general terms. But there is always a danger of unreality in their use. They have their value only if the con-cretes and particulars which they sum up are there at the back of our minds. " For in particulars ", wrote Locke, " our knowledge

[1] *Works* (London, 1854), Vol. I, p. 107.
[2] *Outspoken Essays*, Second Series (Longmans, 1922), p. 113.
[3] *Eth. Nic.*, Bk. VI, Ch. ii, § 5, and Bk. X, Ch. 1, § 4. See my *Modes of Faith* (S.P.C.K., 1934), Ch. II, " Rationalism ", pp. 60, 61. Cp. E. Bevan, *Symbolism and Belief* (Allen and Unwin, 1938), p. 344 : " Reason, I repeat, tells us nothing, but only reason working on the data or experience."
[4] *Science and Method*, tr. Francis Maitland (Nelson), p. 30. Cp. p. 34 : " Mathematics is the art of giving the same name to different things. It is enough that these things, though differing in matter, should be similar in form, to permit of their being, so to speak, run in the same mould."
[5] Swift, *Gulliver's Travels*, Part III, Ch. V, " A Voyage to Laputa."

begins and so spreads itself by degrees to generals." [1] As A. N.
Whitehead reminds us, " Thought is abstract; and the intolerant
use of abstractions is the major vice of the intellect ".[2] We should
remember Pascal's rule always to be prepared mentally to substitute
the definition of a word for the more convenient and shorter word
itself.[3] " The modern mind ", complains Mr. Middleton Murry in
his *The Problem of Style*,

> " is bemused by a cloud of unsubstantial abstractions—Democ-
> racy, Liberty, Revolution, Honour . . . none of the people
> who use these words seem to have the faintest notion what they
> mean or any desire that they should mean anything." [4]

Sometimes, indeed, the case is worse. These abstractions are
often positively misleading. The invention of general terms con-
fuses the minds of their users. They attribute positive existence to
the generalisations of men, and come to think that they are things.
Natural science was seriously retarded when Scientists personified
Nature and declared that " she abhorred a vacuum "; when they
said that fire contained a substance which they called " phlogiston "
and which made things burn; when they thought that they explained the phenomena of weight by saying that it was due to
" attraction ", and when they declared that opium sends you to
sleep because it had a " virtus dormativa ", and that light was a
" luminous movement " mistaking the abstract for the concrete.[5]
Occam, the Nominalist, used what came to be called his " razor "
when he made a clean shave of all these superfluities and declared

---

[1] *Essay concerning the Human Understanding*, Bk. IV, Ch. vii, § 11. Cp.
Bk. IV, Ch. xii, § 3: " Knowledge began in the mind, and was founded
upon particulars; though afterwards, perhaps, no notice was taken thereof,
it being natural for the mind (forward still to enlarge its knowledge) most
attentively to lay up those general notions, and make the proper use of
them, which is to disburden the memory of the cumbersome load of
particulars."

[2] *Science and the Modern World* (Pelican ed., 1939, 1st English ed., 1926),
p. 30.

[3] *Pensées et Opuscules*, ed. Brunschvicg (Hachette), p. 189. " A
substituer toujours mentalement dans la démonstration les définitions
à la place des définis." For the use of this principle see the *Logique de Port
Royal*.

[4] (Oxford, 1922), p. 130.

[5] Cp. T. Huxley, *Science and Christian Tradition*, quoted by A. Headlam
in his *The Miracles of the New Testament* (Murray, 1915), p. 79: " The tena-
city of the wonderful fallacy that the laws of nature are agents instead of
being, as they really are, a mere record of experience upon which we base
our interpretation of what will happen, is an interesting psychological fact,
and would be unintelligible if the tendency of the human mind towards
realism were less strong."

that " *entia non sunt multiplicanda praeter necessitatem* "—that things are not to be multiplied as actually existing unless you must.   Personifications have their uses, but they are dangerous things.[1]   We must avoid mistaking the abstract for the concrete, what A. N. Whitehead calls " the Fallacy of Misplaced Concreteness ". [2]

III

The right to use abstract terms must be earned.   The power to understand general truths must be bought, and often at a high price. Men will readily, for instance, accept the Golden Rule.   It has been uttered by many a moralist, at least in its negative form—by Hillel in the Book of Tobit, by Philo, by Confucius, by Aristotle, by Isocrates, by Epictetus.[3]   Only Christ has effectively called it put into practice.   It means little till the answer is given to the question, " And who is my neighbour? " and the questioner realises that it means, not humanity, but Tom, Dick, and Harry, or any one that he finds who has fallen among thieves.   It surely is a great loss to substitute at the Altar the Summary of the Law for the Decalogue itself, and a still greater loss to replace the Ten Commandments by a *Kyrie Eleison*, the response to the petitions of a vanished Litany, except, perhaps, on a weekday, when the Law of Sinai is itself summed up as a thing familiarly known by weekly repetition on Sunday.

So St. Paul went from particulars to general when he wrote to the Romans:—

> " For this, Thou shalt not commit adultery, thou shalt not kill, thou shalt not steal, thou shalt not covet, and if there be any other commandment it is summed up (A.V. briefly comprehended) in this word, thou shalt love thy neighbour as thyself." [4]

[1] Cp. A. Quiller-Couch, *Studies in Literature*, I, " Classical and Romantic" (Cambridge, 1920), p. 20. After criticising George Brandes' philosophical treatment of English literature with its -isms and tendencies, etc.: " Gentlemen, tell yourself that these foolish abstractions never did any of these foolish things. ' The great artist history.' Call up your courage and say with Betsy Prig that you ' don't believe there is no such person '.   Cure yourselves, if you would be either artists or critics, of this trick of personifying inanities. ' My brethren,' said a clergyman addicted to this foible, ' as we feast and revel catering for the inner man, Septuagesima creeps up to our elbow, and plucking us by the sleeve whispers, " Lent is near ".' Beware, I beg you, of such personifying of what isn't there, whether it be ' the great artist history ', or that minatory virgin Septuagesima."

[2] *Op. cit.*, pp. 56, 66, 74.

[3] Cp. my *Question Time in Hyde Park* (S.P.C.K., 1931), pp. 76, 77.

[4] Rom. xiii, 9.

" In the Churches ", wrote Sir Walter Raleigh in his *On Writing and Writers*,

" or from the philosophers we learn great general principles—the Golden Rule. But the application is left to ourselves to make, with fear and trembling, in each of a thousand diverse occasions as it arises, and it is only when we have made the application for ourselves a thousand times that the general rule comes to have a vital meaning." [1]

IV

So a sermon, as a rule, should have, as Aristotle said a tragedy should have, " a beginning, a middle, and an end ".[2] The beginning or introduction should normally announce a principle and exemplify it by some well-known example from the Gospels. Or it may begin with a text from the words of one of the Evangelists, retold to a point that embodies some great eternal principle. For example, the feeding of the five thousand may be made a starting-point for a sermon on the need of receptivity (as Phillips Brooks made it) ; or on the Eucharist (as St. John shows our Lord using it) ; or on the avoidance of waste (a subject suitable for war-time) ; or on the use of little things (for it was only a lad who had the five barley loaves and the two small fishes) ; or on the need of taking things in order and one at a time (as when " Stir-up " Sunday brings the Christian Year to an end, and we look forward to another and plan for the future) ; or on the need of organisation in religious life (for the men sat down in companies, and did not scramble for the food). In each case the final words of the re-telling would be different.

Then should follow the middle—that which Aristotle said had a beginning before and an end which followed. Examples may follow building up the idea practically. Particular instances may be cited illustrating—that is, making clear—the general principle. Objections may be met throwing up the truth in firm outline. Quotations may be made in which poets and theologians have put in better words what we have been trying to say.

Then, finally, comes the end, after which nothing follows—in words, that is—from the pulpit. The whole has been brought to a single issue and directed to a definite point.

This marriage of abstract and concrete is an element of all good work. It is so with the " structure of the State " as well as with the

[1] *On Writing and Writers* (Arnold, 1926), p. 14.
[2] *Poetics*, Ch. vii, 3, 1450b.

structure of a speech. For, as Aristotle said, " it must of necessity be couched in general terms but our actions deal with particular things ".[1] It is part of the secret of style; Dante, as Dean Church pointed out, " employs without scruple and often with marvellous force of description, any recollection that occurs to him, however homely, of everyday life." [2] Flaubert urged continually that good prose depended on power of exact observation. Hamlet, as Coleridge noted, " who all the play seems reasonable, is only at the last impelled by mere accident to effect his object because his character is the prevalence of the abstracting and generalising habit over the practical." [3] And good old common-sense Paley advised the youthful preacher " to be neither too vague nor too minute ".[4]

V

Jeremy Taylor ended his *Liberty of Prophesying* with a story which he found in one of the Jews' books. I will end with words which I find in one of those of the Greeks. Plato, in his *Statesman*, puts these words into the mouth of the Stranger from Elea :—

> " The higher ideas, my dear Friend, can hardly be set forth except through the medium of examples; every man seems to know all things in a kind of dream, and then again to know nothing when he wakes. . . .

[1] *Politics*, Bk. II, Ch. v, § 12. Cp. *Eth. Nic.*, Bk. II, Ch. vii, § 1, 1107a, tr. H. Rackham (Loeb Library) : " We must not however rest content with stating this general definition, but must show that it applies to the particular virtues. In practical philosophy, although universal principles have a wider application, those covering a particular part of the field possess a higher degree of truth; because conduct deals with particular facts, and our theories are bound to accord with these."

[2] *Dante* (Macmillan, 1893), p. 142. Cp. p. 180: " Words with him are used sparingly, never in play—never because they carry with them poetical recollections—never for their own sake; but because they are instruments which will give the deepest, clearest, sharpest stamp of that image which the poet's mind, piercing to the very heart of his subject, or seizing the characteristic feature which to other men's eyes is confused and lost among others accidental and common, draws forth in severe and living truth."

" Menander ", writing on " The Genius of Dante " in *The Times Literary Supplement* of March 4, 1944, quotes as an instance of concrete imagery. Par. XXII, 1–3, in Italian the words of which Carey's translation are:

> " Astounded, to the guardian of my steps
> I turned me, like the child, who always runs
> Thither for succour, where he trusteth most."

[3] Quoted by A. Quiller-Couch in his *Shakespere's Workmanship* (Benn, 1918, 7th ed., 1930), p. 202.
[4] O. Elton, *op. cit.*, Vol. I, p. 286.

" Can we wonder, then, that the soul has the same uncertainty about the alphabet of things and sometimes and in some cases is firmly fixed by the truth, and then, again, in other cases is all abroad, having somehow or other a correct notion of some combinations; but when they are translated into the long and difficult language of facts, is again ignorant of them." [1]

(Reprinted by permission and with slight additions, from the *Church Times* of September 21, 1945.)

[1] *Politicus*, 278 D, tr. Jowett, ed. 1871, Vol. III, p. 597.

APPENDIX VIII
SUBJECTS OF SUNDAY AFTERNOON LECTURES IN HYDE PARK

DURING sixteen years' experience on Sunday afternoons in Hyde Park the following subjects were treated of, generally in lectures of about half an hour and in sets of four, month by month.

Why Men Believe. The Psychological Groundwork of Apologetics—The Argument from Beauty—The Place of Intellect—The Argument from Experience—The Claim of Authority.

Why We Believe in God. The First Cause Argument—The Arguments from Order and Design—The Moral Argument—The Argument from Revelation and History.

If We Believe in God. Free Will and Determinism—The Problem of Pain—One God, One Law—Theism and Ethics, What Makes a Thing Right—One God, One Self.

Christianity and Conduct. Rights or Duties—Poverty and Waste—Betting and Gambling—Divorce and " Remarriage "—Drink and Alcohol—Why Men do not Go to Church.

The Christian's Claim about Jesus of Nazareth. What the First Christians Thought about Christ—Did Jesus of Nazareth Claim to be Divine?—Is the Claim Credible?—Non-Christian Alternatives, Will they Stand?

The Case for Miracle. Are Miracles Possible?—The Evidence for the Resurrection of Christ—Non-Christian Theories of the Origin of the Belief—The Virgin Birth.

The New Testament. How the First Three Gospels were Written—Who Wrote the Fourth Gospel?—How the Books of the New Testament were Chosen—How we Got our Creeds.

Modes of Faith. Agnosticism. Can we Know?—Rationalism. Is Reason Enough?—Materialism (added later, Sentimentalism). (Is Feeling Sufficient?). Is Matter All?—Dualism. Mind and Matter—Atheism and Theism. What do we Mean by God?—Institutionalism. Need we have a Church?—Sacramentalism. Outward Signs and Invisible Grace—Catholicism, For All Places, All Times, and All Men—Creeds and Customs. What Each Stands for.

I   115

Evolution of Man. Evolution and the Fall—Evolution of the Idea of God—Evolution of Morals.

The Things that Matter. The Spirit of Envy—Rights or Duties—Rule or Service?

(Most of the above have been written out and published in book form by the S.P.C.K.)

Single Lectures

Immortality—The Atonement—Free Will in History—Comparative Religion.

What do we Mean by Faith?—Can't a Man be Good without going to Church?—The Argument from Silence (with illustrations from popular anti-Christian Propaganda)—How do we Know that Christ Ever Existed?—Science and Religion—Isn't Christianity a Business?—The Sort of Things People Say—The Codex Siniaticus.

(Several of the above have been published by the S.P.C.K. in its " Little Books on Religion " Series.)

At a " Padre's Hour "

Evolution and Genesis—How the Book of Genesis was Compiled—Astronomy and the Infinitely Great—Chemistry and the Infinitely Small—Man in the Middle is what Matters.

Single Lectures

Prediction and Prophecy—Spiritualism—Poetry and Story in Religion (with illustrations).

Written or Planned but not Delivered

The Doctrine of the Trinity. How the Doctrine Arose—The Problem on Unity and Diversity—The Scale of Creation from Matter to Man.

Humanism, True and False. The Mystery of Man—Stoic and Epicurean—In the Ancient World—In the Modern World—Man, Social and Individual.

APPENDIX IX

THE LITERATURE OF PREACHING

THE literature of preaching is enormous in quantity, but much of it is slight in value. The subject is often treated merely for its historical interest. When it has a practical aim it is often inadequately dealt with as just one part of Pastoral Theology, itself not very scientifically studied. Moreover, the conditions under which it was produced have so changed that its chief use is to make us ask how it must be contrasted with what is needed to-day and what may be learned from other departments of church work (of which it is one), so that the most useful course for our practical needs would seem to be to study parallel arts and sciences such as rhetoric, style, education, psychology and elocution.

I. THE LITERATURE OF PREACHING

(1) Standard works of reference give us little help. The *Encyclopaedia Britannica* has a short article on " Preaching " which is little more than a list of the names of preachers; useful, perhaps, to give their dates and place them in historical order. The *Encyclopaedia of Religion and Ethics* has a longer article of the same sort. E. C. Dargan's *History of Preaching* (New York, 1905) is a standard work of the same order; and provides material for showing how different churches and conditions have been in other ages. But it does little more.

G. R. Owst's *Preaching in Mediaeval England, an Introduction to Sermon MSS. of the period 1350 to 1450,* " Cambridge Studies in Mediaeval Life and Thought " (Cambridge, 1926), is a first-class work, critically and interestingly set forth. His *Literature and Pulpit in Mediaeval England* (1933) is " an attempt made to estimate comprehensively the debt of English Literature to the message of her Mediaeval Church " as a whole. Both have been drawn upon by Canon Charles Smyth in his *The Art of Preaching, A Practical Survey of Preaching in the Church of England, 747–1939* A.D. (S.P.C.K., 1940), to guide us in our problems to-day.

(2) As part of the whole duty of the clergy there is much to be found in general books on Parish Work, in Bishops' Charges,

Visitation Sermons, etc. There is a chapter on " The Parson Preaching " in George Herbert's *Priest to the Temple, or The Countrey Parson* (1632), Jeremy Taylor's *Works* (Vol. I, pp. 107–111) include his *Rules and Advices to the Clergy of Down and Connor* given in 1661, which contain " IV. Rules and advice concerning preaching ". Gilbert Burnet, in 1661, wrote his *Discourse on the Pastoral Care*, with its ninth chapter " Concerning Preaching ". These and several others from the eighteenth century were collected and republished in *The Clergyman's Instructor*, by the Clarendon Press in 1807, which became a sort of general manual of Pastoral Theology, reprinted several times in the early part of the nineteenth century, and can often be picked up second-hand. They are full of quaint saying and shrewd advice which should supply material for an interesting paper on ideals of preaching and its place in public worship and church work generally in the post-Reformation Church of England. But the only work that has permanent value in homiletics is perhaps chapters 18–22 of Hooker's *Ecclesiastical Polity*, Bk. V, which treat of the place of the Lessons and the Sermon in Morning and Evening Prayer on principles which do not change.

(3) The need of such books on parish work in general, and on preaching in particular, was felt in the last part of the nineteenth century, but (owing to the amateurishness of the study of Pastoral Theology generally) it was not met as part of the general study of theology at the Universities, but by asking famous preachers to come and give occasional courses on preaching. In 1877 Phillips Brooks, the Rector of Trinity Church in Boston, Mass., U.S.A., gave his *Lectures on Preaching delivered at Yale College* (Macmillan, 1877), which were followed, year by year, by many similar courses, which fill the shelves of Theological Libraries and second-hand booksellers. They are all much the same, and repeat the same excellent commonplaces that their hearers could quite easily have told themselves— that the preacher should be a good man, should study theology, should be a man of character, should speak naturally in the pulpit, should say his prayers, with generally a chapter at the end saying he may read novels and sometimes take a holiday. They are given by people, as a rule, who had already become famous by their natural gifts and had had no experience of teaching others who found preaching less easy. The lecturers have generally got into the habit of preaching, and do so when they lecture. They have a certain value in keeping up the interest of the preacher in his work, but when you have read one you have read them all. One of the latest of these which has been found useful and makes a real attempt to

supply what is needed is *Lectures on Preaching and Sermon Construction* by Paul Bull, C.R. (S.P.C.K., 1928).

So, perhaps, the best general introduction to the literature of preaching will be found in the relevant chapters and the bibliographies of *The Cambridge History of English Literature* (which should be in every Public Library), Vol. VIII, Ch. xii, " Divines of the Church of England, 1660–1700 "; Vol. X, *The Age of Johnson*, Ch. xv, " Divines ", Ch. xvi, " Dissent "; Vol. XII, *The Nineteenth Century*, Ch. xii, " The Oxford Movement ", Ch. xiii, " The Growth of Liberal Theology ". These are historical studies, written by specialists, with the same standards of criticism that are applied to secular writers, and putting sermons, as well as other theological works, into their right place in English literature as a whole.

II. RHETORIC. THE ART OF PERSUADING OTHERS

A more profitable study will therefore be the consideration of the nature of rhetoric, the art of persuading others, as distinct from dialectic and logic, the arts by which we discover the truths that rhetoric aims at diffusing. Socrates was the originator of the method of dialectic and Plato elaborated his practice as an art, while Aristotle systematised both by examining their permanent and fundamental laws. Our modern European civilisation is mainly based on the work of ancient Greece. Sermons are a special form of rhetoric.

(1) The relevant passages about its nature will be found running through the whole of Plato's writings, especially in the *Republic* and the *Gorgias* and in the last part of the *Phaedrus*. Some of the chief features of the difference of spoken and written language were discussed in his Letter vii (if it was by Plato), tr. by R. G. Bury in the Loeb Library of Classical Authors, Greek Writers. Aristotle's *Poetics* elaborate the art of writing, chiefly over Greek Tragedy, while his *Rhetoric* is based on the practice of the Courts. It can be conveniently studied in Greek and in English in the Loeb Library, together with Longinus' *On the Sublime* and Demetrius' *On Style*, which did so much to create the mental atmosphere in which the Gospel was first preached, in which Origen taught and Chrysostom preached. Cicero's *De Oratore*, his *Tusculan Disputations* and his *Brutus* should be read, though they are of less value in themselves, as his object was largely just to show that his native Latin could talk philosophy as well as Greek. His works are based on the practice of the Roman law courts, for which, later on, Augustine trained

his pupils at Rome and Milan, and on which he based his own
preaching after his conversion, and his *De Doctrina Christiana* (*Op.* iii.),
which he wrote for his clergy in Africa. But it is doubtful whether
much practical help can be gained from times when conditions in
the Church were so different. Whately's *Elements of Rhetoric*
(7th ed., 1866, and often reprinted), inspired largely by Aristotle and
" designed principally for the instruction of unpractised writers ",
is still valuable.

(2) We may go on to the study of sermons. But few of those of
great preachers have won place in the world's literature. Chrysostom, Augustine, Bossuet, Jeremy Taylor, Tillotson, South, Butler
(ed. J. H. Bernard, Vol. I [Macmillan, 1900, 4*s.* 6*d.*]), Newman,
nearly exhaust the list and, except perhaps in the case of Bossuet and
Butler, their other writings rank higher. Sermons were made to be
heard, not read. In the case of Butler it is their philosophical
importance that has made their fame. The French preachers of
the seventeenth century find a place in histories of literature such
as G. Lanson's *Histoire de la Litterature française* (Hachette, 17th ed.,
1922), IVme Partie, " Les grands artistes classiques ", Livre iii, Ch. vi,
" Bossuet et Bourdaloue ", and among the *Grands Écrivains Classiques
Français*. Liddon framed his preaching on the model of Bossuet;
but it is doubtful whether the modern preacher would get much help
from the study of Tillotson or Wesley. Still, it would be useful to work
through a volume of selected great sermons such as Bishop Hensley
Henson's *Selected English Sermons, 16th–19th Centuries*, No. 464 in the
Oxford " World's Classics " (3*s.*), to try to discover wherein their
greatness lies, and to see what modern preaching can learn from
their examples.

(3) Meanwhile the training of the clergy must be largely self-
training on the lines laid down in the Theological College. Sermons
that have been found useful for study there have been those of
Liddon (*e.g.*, " Christ in the Storm "); of F. W. Robertson of
Brighton, especially for his introductions and twofold development
of the subject (*e.g.*, his " Zacchaeus ", " The Scepticism of Pilate ",
" Christ's Judgment concerning Inheritance "); of J. H. Newman,
for their terseness, understanding of human nature, clear, coherent
structure, and simple and beautiful language, *e.g.*, " The Religious
Use of Excited Feelings " (*Parochial Sermons*, Vol. I, Serm. 9); and
of Phillips Brooks of Boston, U.S.A., especially for his introductions,
e.g., " Make the Men Sit Down " (*Twenty Sermons*, Serm. 13).

III. STYLE. THE ART OF WRITING

There is an essential difference between spoken and written words. The art of speech came before the art of writing. Plato preferred the flexibility of dialectic to the fullness of written language. All writing should be based on common speech, and sermons should be written with an audience in mind. The preliminary task of preaching is a discipline that produces what is, in writing, called style.

(1) The preacher should carry on what he learned at school in the form of grammar, and should continually be interesting himself in the niceties of its higher uses. He will do well to keep his critical faculties alert by reading from time to time a few pages of H. W. and F. G. Fowler's *The King's English* and of the former's *Dictionary of Modern English Usage* (Oxford, 1908 and 1926, 7*d.* 6*d.*). This will help him to finish his sentences, avoid false concords, keep clear of jargon and get his " wills " and " shalls " right, not saying " I would like " when he means " I should like ". The experience of school teaching should be utilised for self-teaching by using such a book as P. J. Hartog and A. H. Langdon's *The Writing of English* (Oxford, 1907, 2*s.* 6*d.*). A more recent work, recommended as " provocative ", is G. T. Warner's (formerly master on the Modern Side at Harrow) *On the Writing of English* (Blackie, Edinburgh). *The Teaching of English in England*, being the report of the Departmental Committee appointed by the Board of Education to inquire into the position of English in the Educational System of England (H.M. Stationery Office, Imperial House, Kingsway, 1921, 1*s.* 6*d.*), will show what is being done in the schools of the country.

(2) This leads us on to the question of style, in which we have so much to learn from the French. The great French preachers Bossuet, Bourdaloue, Fénelon, etc., made their mark at a time when the question of style was being much discussed. Pascal, it has been said, fixed the style of French in his *Provinciales*, and the first chapter of his *Pensées* in Brunschvicg's edition, now generally accepted for reference, is " Pensées sur l'Esprit et sur le Style " (Hachette's *Classiques Français*, p. 317). Cp. his " Opuscule " *De l'Esprit Géométrique*, Section ii, " De l'Art de Persuader " (p. 185). Bouleau's *L'Art Poétique*, largely based on Horace's *Ars Poetica* (1674), led on to Buffon's *Discours sur le style*, " pronounced at the French Academy on the Day of his Reception as a member in 1753 ", the source of the famous quotation " Le style est (de) l'homme même ", which is a classic on the subject.

(3) Books like R. L. Stevenson's *Essays in the Art of Writing* (Chatto and Windus, 1905), Walter Pater's *Appreciations, with an Essay on Style* (Macmillan, 1893, reprinted 1924), Sir Walter Raleigh's *Style* (Arnold, 1918), Sir Arthur Quiller-Couch's *The Art of Writing* (Cambridge, 1916) and *The Art of Reading* (1920, Pocket Edition 3s. 6d., 1934, and many times reprinted) and many similar books, will serve to keep the preacher's consciousness of style alert.

A more modern book is *English Prose Style* (Bell, 1928, 7th ed., 1942) by Herbert Read, who deals in Part I with composition and in Part II with rhetoric, and illustrates his theses with many examples, making the book an anthology of quotations. *Rhetoric and English Composition* by H. J. C. Grierson (Oliver and Boyd, Edinburgh and London, 1944) is another excellent and suggestive work. See also the publications of the English Association (Sec., 3 Cromwell Place, London, S.W.7).

IV. EDUCATION. THE ART OF TEACHING

(1) In education generally we should study what is the same whether its subject is religious or secular. Questions of interest and attention are common to both. The proper length of a sermon and a lesson are governed by the same general rules of effort and fatigue. The alternation of passive reception with active discovery should be found in both, though in school the latter is by discussion and experiment; and in church by participation in the Liturgy and the singing of hymns, while discussion must be arranged for elsewhere.

The form of the lesson will follow some modification of the Herbartian " five steps ": while the outline of the sermon will be some development of Aristotle's " beginning, middle, and end ". The planning of the School Syllabus will give useful suggestion for formal courses of sermons or, perhaps more profitably, for continuity of teaching in the mind of the preacher.

General books on the teacher's craft are many. A. Pinsent's *The Principles of Teaching Method* (London, 1941), A. G. Hughes and E. H. Hughes' *Learning and Teaching : an Introduction to Psychology* (London, 1937), have been widely recommended to students in Training Colleges. Valentine Davis *The Science and Art of Teaching* (Cartwright and Rattray Ltd., Hyde, Manchester, and London, 1930) contains much that is irrelevant to homiletics, but is just the book to give suggestions in many ways. The Oxford University Department of Education publishes a very full *Select Bibliography* arranged under different headings (15, Norham Gardens, Oxford,

6*d.*), and in any Public Library there would probably be found a shelf of books on education that have been found useful.

(2) The use of illustration by stories need not be restricted to the New Testament parables; and quotations in poetry or prose often serve to illustrate or drive home the preacher's words.   Sermons are for adults; and from the Adult Education Movement and from the activities of the Workers' Educational Association there is much for the preacher to learn.   J. J. Findlay's *Principles of Class Teaching* (Macmillan, 1907) and J. Adams' *Exposition and Illustration in Teaching* (Macmillan, 1909) are two such books that have proved their worth.   The latter's admirable little *Primer of Teaching, with special reference to Sunday-School Work* in T. and T. Clark's " Bible Class Primers " (1903, 1*s.*) by the manner in which he applies the principles worked out in such manuals to the special conditions of the Sunday School will suggest to the preacher how they can be applied to those of the pulpit.   For adapting them to adolescents and adults T. H. Pear's *The Maturing Mind* and A. J. J. Ratcliff's *The Adult Class* (both in Nelson's series of " Discussion Books", 1938, 3*s.*) will be found valuable.   The latter has a useful final chapter on " Further Reading ".

(3) There remains the question of the self-training of the schoolmaster in the classroom and of the priest in the pulpit.   This should be studied in the light of normal psychology.   The problems of abnormality are for the specialist rather than for the teacher and preacher.   W. James' *Talks to Teachers* (Longmans, 1922) is still useful and suggestive.   The place of subconscious action after study, the need first of steady reading followed by " incubation ", the way in which ideas suddenly come up again in a new form that is our own, the importance of recording them at once for use in sermons, the impossibility of preaching satisfactorily unless sermons are on the stocks for more than a week, should all be considered.   A useful work on this is Graham Wallas' *The Art of Thought* (Cape, 1927, 4*s.* 6*d.*).

V. ELOCUTION.   THE ART OF SPEECH

· There remains for consideration the part that sound plays in ordinary speech, in oratory and in the kindred arts of class teaching, song, and drama.   Conversation is the basis not only of style in writing (as we saw above) but of all formal or elaborated diction. But it seems to need the living voice of a teacher of elocution to train it, and that little can be done by books beyond what can be found in the few pages of those mentioned above.

(1) The teaching of elocution must therefore be mainly self-teaching. (The chief use of even the good tutor would seem to be that he induces his pupils to practise, since they do not want to pay fees for nothing.) The student should train himself to hear what he reads even when reading silently, and should get out of the habit of reading by the eye alone. He should practise reading poetry and plays, hearing in them the sound of his own voice, noting the difference of poetry and prose, and marking how many different things the same words may be made to express. He would do well to get someone else to work with him, each reading, say, poems from *The Golden Treasury* and passages from Shakespeare ending with Hamlet's "Speech to the Players" (Act III, Sc. ii) with one another, and discussing their various interpretations. This should be done first in an ordinary room and then in a big hall or school-room, using passages from sermons, in the pulpit in church, taking care that the pronunciation and phrasing of the words are not altered in the larger place. The highly artificial result will then sound " natural ".

(2) There is one field, however, where great help can be obtained from books. The scientific study of speech-sounds or phonetics has been elaborated for teaching foreign languages, and is no less valuable for learning to speak our own. Its use in homiletics is first to analyse exactly how its various sounds are made, and so to make a speaker " mouth-conscious ". Then he should practise with " tongue-twisters " and passages difficult to enunciate clearly, and go on till correct speech formation becomes automatic, so that he need not think about it in the pulpit or at the Altar. In books on phonetics there are generally a few pages about the mechanism of the voice, deep breathing, stress, pitch and phrasing, and the difference of public speaking and conversation, etc.

Perhaps the best book on phonetics is W. Ripman's *The Sounds of Spoken English,* first published in 1905, re-written and enlarged in 1914, many times reprinted and added to out of practical experience in teaching, and re-issued in 1931 under the title of *English Phonetics* (Dent, 2nd ed., 1934) with a good bibliography in Appendix VIII.

(3) When the student has mastered the elements of phonetics he is in the position to consider the question of written or extempore sermons. The written sermon at least gives a guarantee that the preacher has taken trouble and does not, when he gets into the pulpit, merely say the first thing that comes into his head. But bad delivery may kill a well-composed sermon even if written with an audience in mind. The preacher must be able to deliver a sermon

exactly as it stands in his MS., and to do so in such a way that the greater part of his congregation will not know if it was written or not.

A few general rules may be noted. At the end of a sentence he should drop his voice in pitch, but not in force. He should slightly over-articulate when the matter is unfamilar to his congregation, as in the changing parts of the Liturgy. He should know how to stop coughing by a slight pause, but without calling attention to the cougher. He should realise, especially if speaking in the open air, that the lower registers of the voice carry best. He should hold up his head and look at the back rows of the congregation, only lowering his eyes to his MS. He must see that the desk is high enough before going into the pulpit and find out beforehand how to turn on the light, etc., but all these " tips " can be got into a few pages of a good book on phonetics, or supplied by common sense.

(4) Problems similar to those of the preacher are met in other professions. Books on teaching (such as those mentioned above) generally contain good advice about the use of the voice and the importance of right gesture and bearing in the handling of a class. The B.B.C. has shown that written announcements can be made to sound quite natural and that even untrained speakers can be coached so as to sound nearly so.

The quality of the voice plays a great part in oratory. Good singers generally have pleasant speaking voices also. Preachers should try to acquire a pleasant tone and should " sing into their voices ". They should never shout or strain their voices, or try to sing above the pitch that is natural to them, or to make their voices heard in competition with a noisy organ. Even trained singers seem often to be quite ignorant of phonetics, and excellent conductors of choirs will give advice which is glaringly wrong. The problems of the singer are excellently treated by H. Plunket Greene in his *Interpretation in Song* (Macmillan's " Musicians' Library ", London, 1912). On the stage a similar problem has to be faced. Mephistopheles was wrong when he said that a parson could only learn from an actor if he too was a comedian, but probably stage experience would be more useful in directing the disposition and movement of a choir in the chancel and of the ceremonies of the Altar than in the art of elocution, which has been well studied apart from the stage.

(Reprinted by permission, and with additions, from Leaflet 185, April, 1946, Central Society of Sacred Study.)

INDEX

"Absente auxilio perquirimus undique frustra,
Sed nobis ingens indicis auxilum est."

(Without a key we search and search in vain,
But a good index is a monstrous gain.)

King's Dictionary of Classical and Foreign Quotations, Adespota No. 3019, p. 387.

ABBREVIATIONS, to be fixed, 11
Abstract and Concrete. *See* Generals and Particulars.
Adams, J., "curve of attention," 34
Advent, sermons for, 54
Alice through the Looking-Glass :
  advice of the White Queen on note-taking, 8
All Saints' Day, sermon for, 53
All Souls' Day, sermon for, 54
Amiel, H. F., teaching oneself by teaching others, 58
Anselm, St., using wax tablets, 6
Anthroposophy, 48, 61
Apologetics:
  to be prepared for, 62
  subjects treated in Hyde Park, 115–116
Apperception mass, 41
Aristotle:
  animals unable to reason, 19
  Athenian law courts, xiv
  "beginning, middle, and an end," 29
  deep voice of the high-minded man, 76
  Ethics, recommended by Bp. King, 47
  Generals and Particulars, 107 *n.*
  method of delivery, 64
  number three, 18
  true theories useful, 109
  speech the prerogative of man alone, 65 *n.*
  systematic writer on rhetoric, 83
  three points to study, 1
Arnold, M., memory's tablets, 1
Art of letter-writing, Mrs. Turner's, 37
Athanasius, St., "tam modico flexu vocis," 81
Atonement, unsatisfactory sermon on, 45
Atterbury, Dr., Dean Swift on exhortation defeating its own end, 35 *n.*
Aubrey, John, on Hobbes and "thoughts darting," 5

Augustine, St. :
  quotes Cicero, 20
  De Doctrina Christiana, 83
  the right hand of God, 54
  "tam modico vocis inflexione," 81
"Aut Deus aut homo non bonus," 60
Authorised Version. *See* Bible

Bacon, on common-place books, 40
Baptism in the Early Church, 55
Beatitudes and moral theology, 57
Berkeley, "things particular and concrete," 106
Bible, The, Authorised and Revised Versions, 28, 67–68, 84
Blake, W., "in minute particulars," 108
Boileau, "learn to think ere you pretend to write," 18
Books, analyse when reading, 22
Brains Trust:
  anticipating questions, 62
  ignorance of theology, 41
British Association, inaudibility at meetings, 69 *n.*
Brontë, Charlotte, Jane Eyre and German, 66–67
Brooks, Phillips, Sermons:
  the man with one talent, 52
  the man with two talents, 51
  Make the Men Sit Down, 32 *n.*, 79, 102–105
Browne, Sir Thomas, 53 *n.*
Browning, Robert:
  Pippa Passes, 52
  "the thrush's first fine careless rapture," 8
Buchan, John, the German language, 66 *n.*
Buffon:
  style and balance of ideas, 20
  style, the man himself, 39, 89–93
Burgon, Dean, visit to Dr. Routh, 4 *n.*

Calvert, Louis, stage elocution, 69 n.
Cardinal virtues and moral theology, 58
Carroll, Lewis, " what I tell you three times," 29
Cartwright, confused noise of the people, 68
Case for Miracle, the Resurrection, 61
Case for Christianity, the Right Hand of God, 54
Catholicism, English, and All Saints' Day, 53
" Christ " or " Chroist " ? 78
Christian Doctrine, Report of Commission on, 52
Church, Dean R. W.:
    on Dante and style, 113
    Hooker and English prose, 67
Cicero:
    Brutus, 83
    citation of examples, 33 n.
    Demosthenes, use of voice, 77 n.
    rhetoricians of his day, xiv
    on " the man of eloquence," 20
Classes, need of, to supplement sermons, 45
Clement of Alexandria, " the finger of God," 54
Coins, experiment with, 24
Coleridge, on Hamlet, 113
Commonplace Books:
    to be avoided, 10
    Bacon on value of, 40
Communion, continual harping on, 49
Confirmation, sermon on and methods of preparation for, 49
Conversational style, 69
Courses of sermons, 4, 45 ff., 97–98
Cowper, " friendly and agreeable conversations," 82 n.
Cranford:
    Miss Deborah's letters, 107
    old ladies of, 66
Cull, Richard, on Garrick, 68 n.
Curve of attention, 34
Cuttle, Captain, 1, 8

Dante, use of words, 113
Demosthenes, " robicosity," 73, 76
Descartes, clear ideas, 30 n.
Dickens, Captain Cuttle, 1, 8
Diogenes Lærtius, on Demosthenes, 76 n.
Drummond, Henry, Natural Law in the Spiritual World, 59

Eadmer, Life of Anselm, 6
Easter Day, sermon on, 61
Edersheim, Dr., on the " Unjust Steward," 33 n.

Education:
    Christianity the chief factor in, 63
    self, 47–53
Eliot, George, " a sermon quite finished," 106
English:
    beauty of, 65–67
    as a universal language, 84
English Church, " not producing saints," 53
Eyre, Jane, the German language, 66
Examples, illustration by, 33
Expression work, 31, 34

Faust. See Goethe
Fichte, educational theory and two classes of student, 31
Findlay, J. J., on Herbart, 31
Flaubert, on exact observation, 113
Francis of Assisi, St., the Fioretti, 60
Free Will:
    and Determinism, 45–46
    and Foreknowledge, 48
Fuller, Thomas, " men of middle and moderate parts," 51
Funeral customs, need for sermons on, 50

Garrick's Mode of Reading the Liturgy, 68, 72
Generals and Particulars, 106–114
George Herbert on, 3, 33
Goethe:
    " eben wo Begriffe fehlen," 14
    " ein Komödiant könnt einen Pfarrer lehren," 64, 83
    " Ich kann das Predigt nicht vertragen," 106
    " was du ererbt," 40
    " wenn ihr's nicht fühlt," 12 n.
Golden Rule, 111–112
Gospel for the day, preaching on, 1–3

Herbert, George:
    an hour the unit, 43 n.
    illustration by stories, 33 n.
    " in a huddling or slubbering fashion," 68
    " judge not the preacher," 59 n.
Hobbes, thoughts darting, 5, 7
Honest Dealing included on the eighth Commandment, 58
Hooch, De, composition in his picture, 26 n.
Hooker, Richard:
    " indigested prayers ", 68
    opening sentence analysed, 23–24
    on sacramentalism, 49

Hooker, Richard (*contd.*):
" showing what English prose might be," 67
" tam modico vocis inflectione," 81
" unlimited generalities," 108
Homer, first, next, and last of all, 18
Horace, " si vis me flere," 12
Hort, F. J. A., on the Revised Version, 68 *n.*
Hour, an, " the unit of attention," 42–3
Housman, A. C., writing poetry, 7–8
Huxley, T. H., laws of nature, 110 *n.*
Hymns:
choice of, after the sermon, 34
four- or eight-line verses, 27
how to be sung, 86 ff
to be pitched low, 75–76, 125
Welsh, 27, 87

Ignatius of Antioch, " beginning to be a disciple ", 43
Ignatius Loyala, method of Meditation, 31–32
Illingworth, J. R., on Episcopacy, 55 *n.*
Illustration by stories, 33
Immortality, sermon on, 48, 54
Incubation, 4–8
Inge, W. R., people moved by abstractions, 109
Intelligence, not to be under-estimated, 32
Introductions to sermons useful for practice, 32, 79, 102–105

James-Lange, theory, 77 *n.*
James, William, brain-paths, 20
Johnson, Dr.:
advice about fine writing, 22
and Johnsonese, 107
ignorance of congregation, 41, 106
" I hope not," to Mr. Walker, 72
reading strong though low, 76 *n.*
on gesticulation, 77 *n.*
reading with a commentary, 47
Jongleur de Nôtre Dame, 80
Joubert:
carrying about a note book, 8
getting a picture and working out details, 4
to teach is to learn twice, 48
Jourdain, M., " *Mais je dis, O,*" 71
Jowett, B., " Christ whom we have not seen," 60 *n.*

Kames, Lord, on Shakespere's language, 107
Karma, injustice of, 62
Keats, nothing real till experienced, 12

Kempis, Thomas à:
personal attachment to Christ, 60
heaven where God is, 54 *n.*
Kenyon, Sir Frederic, nothing to fear from research, 44–45
King, Bp., study of moral theology, 47
King's College:
sermon writing and pastoral theology, xiv
elocution, training in, 72 ff.
Knowledge, never to be assumed, 32

Lamb, Charles, Shakespeare and Christ, 60
Langlois, M. Victor, use of note books, 9–10
Latham, H., the " unjust " steward, 33 *n.*
Laudatores temporis acti, 16, 61
Lear, King, Cordelia's voice, 76
Letter-writing, Jane Taylor, 37
Liddon, H. P., Sermon on Christ in the Storm, 33, 79
Lingua franca, claim of English to be, 84
Locke, knowledge begins with particulars, 109–110
London, " are you going to—to-morrow? " five possible meanings, 70
Looking ahead in Parish Work, 1–3, 41
Lowell, H. R., All Saints' Day, 53 *n.*
Lucidity, depends on seeing a pattern, 20 ff.

McNeile, E. R. (Sister Rhoda), on Theosophy, 62 *n.*
Mackenzie, Dr. J. S., purpose of punishment, 55 *n.*
Magazine, Parish, to reinforce the work of sermons, 46
Marriage, need for sermons on, 50
Massanet, the Jongleur de Nôtre Dame, 80
May, Phil, his method in drawing, 22
Meditation, not to be used for a homileletic end, 31–32
Meeting on Monday, the longer span of work, 1–2, 40 ff.
" Menander ", " The Genius of Dante," 113
Méré, Chevalier de:
and Pascal, 6
the " honnête homme," 53
Milton, his faith and morals, 84
Miracles do not happen, 61
Modern Churchman, The, article on fore-knowledge and free-will, 48 *n.*
Monday, meeting on, to arrange the work for the week, 1–2, 40 ff.

Moore, Geo., *The Brook Kerith*, 61
Mulcaster, Richard, on the English "tung," 67
Murry, Middleton, style and "unsubstantial abstractions," 110
Music, triple time in, 26

Napoleon, story of, 60
Natural voice, 75 ff.
Newman, J. H.:
 definition of a gentleman, 53
 use of excited feelings, 79
 Whateley, debt to, 83
Nicene Creed, " God *of* God," etc., 71
Nicole, story of Pascal, 7

Occam's " razor ", removing abstracts, 110
Oxford English Dictionary, use of slips, 9

Padre's Hour, subjects for, 99–101
Paley, " neither too vague nor too minute," 113
Palgrave, *The Golden Treasury*, 74
Parish work, its relation to sermons, 46
Pascal:
 definitions to be substituted for the things defined, 110 *n.*
 " sustained eloquence," 35
 " fair deeds hidden," 54 *n.*
 " the matter newly put," 13
 " le moi," 38
 " using a note-book," 7
 style based on common speech, 34 *n.*
 text the last thing chosen, 36
 " the right hand of God," 54
Pater, Walter:
 " come unto Me," 81–82
 on style, 21 *n.*
Pattern in a sermon, 24 ff.
Pattison, Mark, on Hooker's style, 24
Personification, " that minatory virgin Septuagesima," 111
Pestalozzi, educational theories, 31
Perorations, appeal to feeling, 34
Phlogiston, making things burn, 110
Phonetics, study of, 73, 124 ff.
Pictures, and the " Rule of Three," 25
Pitch of voices to be low, 75–76, 125
Plato:
 on examples, 113–114
 on preludes, 32
Poincaré, Henri:
 algebraic formulæ, 109
 how sudden thoughts came, 7
Press; letters to, supplementing sermons, 46
Pronoun, first personal, 38
Psychology and sermons, 83

Punch, omission of " h " unaccented, 69 *n.*
Punishment, purpose of, 54–55

Quarterly Review, " The Good Old Times," 16
Question Time in Hyde Park, 41, 46 *n.*, 83, 111 *n.*, 115–116
Quiller-Couch, A.:
 personification and Septuagesima, 111
 quotes Coleridge, 113 *n.*
Quintilian, and Education, xiv, 83
Quotations, 13

Raleigh, Sir Walter:
 the Golden Rule, 112
 " triptology," 30 *n.*
Rationalist Press Association:
 arguments to be met, 33
 propaganda to be anticipated, 63
Real Presence, to be considered in a sermon, 49
Reading kept up by sermon preparation, 47
Rembrandt, picture of the Syndics, 25–26
Reporters' note-books to be avoided, 10
Revised Version. *See* Bible
Reynolds, Sir Joshua, the grand style in painting, 107
Rhoda, Sister, and Theosophy, 62 *n.*
" Right Hand of God " in the Fathers, 54
Rights or duties, 56
Ripman, W., English phonetics and tongue-twisters, 73, 124
Rivarol, Antoine:
 thought as speech hiding itself, 19
 what is not clear is not French, 65
 " Robicosity " and Demosthenes, 76
Robertson, F. W.:
 " Triumph over Hindrances," 33, 79
 " Christ's Judgement Concerning Inheritance," 33 *n.*, 79
Routh, Dr., verify your references, 4
" Rule of Three," 24–32
Russell, Bertrand, speech an art, 75

Sacramentalism, considered thoroughly, 49
Sainte Beuve, on Pascal, 7 *n.*
Schools, Church, need of supplementing preaching by, 46
Seaman, Owen, Victorian ballads, 26
Selden, John, " talking oratoriously," xiii *n.*
Sermons:
 few as literature, 82
 giving point to study, 47
 learning from allied arts, 83 ff.

Sermons (*contd.*):
  self-education, 47
  subjects not treated in, 50
  suitable language for, 34
  three months plan, 52 ff., 94–98
Shakespeare:
  pieces chosen for practice, 77–78
  Hamlet, his tablets, 1
  Hamlet, generalising habit, 113
  " the tongue that he spake," 84
Shaw, Bernard, our ill-dressed language, 67
Sheridan:
  Art of Reading, 68
  reading low, 76
Sight, in French and German thought, 64–67
Smyth, Charles, *The Art of Preaching*, 82, 117
Socrates, demagogues hiring men with fine, loud, persuasive voices, 71
Sonnet, structure in fours and threes, 26
Span of work, 41 ff.
Spectator, The, letter in, 3
Speech, an art, 75, 123
Steward, of unrighteousness, 33
Stories:
  as illustrations, 14, 33
  as introductions, 32
Study Circles, supplementary to sermons, 46
Style:
  in balance of ideas, 6–7, 20, 39, 89–93
  Walter Pater on, 21
Suicide, need for sermons on, 50
Swift:
  the men of Laputa, 109
  " Pulpit Eloquence," 35 *n.*, 64
Symbols, to be fixed in taking notes, 11

" Tab " note-books, entries in, at time of writing, 12
Tacitus, borrowing from others, 40
Talents, the man with two, 51
Taylor, Jane, method of writing, 37
Taylor, Jeremy:
  Abstract and Concrete, 3 *n.*
  " generals not explicated," 42, 108–109
  Holy Living, 57
  Liberty of Prophesying, 113
Ten Commandments:
  loss if the Golden Rule is substituted, 111–112
  moral theology of, 58

Tennyson, " truth embodied in a tale," 14
Text, often the last chosen, 36
Times, The, articles of three paragraphs, 29
" Tongue-twisters," 73
Training for the Ministry, 106 *n.*

Universal language, 67, 84

Veni Creator, " dextra Dei tu digitus," 54
Verify your references in popular publications, 62–63
Verse, and the " Rule of Three," 26
Victorian ballads, 26
Visualization, power of, in English thought, 30 *n.*
Voice, the natural, 69, 75, 79

Walker, Mr., teaching elocution, 72
Wallas, Graham:
  " fringe thoughts," 5
  salesmanship, 71
  The Art of Thought, 2 *n.*
Walpole, Horace, on Dr. Johnson's " triptology," 30
Ward, Mrs. Humphry, and Walter Pater, 81–82
Welsh hymns, their structure, 27, 87
Wesley, Charles, Communion hymns, 49
Westcott, Dr., not recognising any syncretism in Egypt, 62–63
Whateley, Richard:
  on Aristotle, 83
  " and there was light," 70
  Newman's debt to, 83–84
  rhetoric no substitute for conviction, 39 *n.*
  " for unpracticed writers," xiv
  on Sheridan's *Art of Reading*, 68 *n.*
  tone of conversation, 82 *n.*
  " transplanting from other writers," 57 *n.*
Whitehead, Prof. A. N.:
  intolerant of the use of abstractions, 110
  " fallacy of misplaced concreteness," 111
Words, meaning of technical, to be learned, 42
Wordsworth:
  Happy Warrior, 53
  " the inward eye," 65
  lines on Lucy, 71
  Sonnet on Milton, 84

PRINTED AND BOUND IN GREAT BRITAIN BY RICHARD CLAY AND COMPANY, LTD.,
BUNGAY, SUFFOLK.